COMMITTED

COMMITTED

A RABBLE-ROUSER'S MEMOIR

Dan Mathews

ATRIA BOOKS
New York   London   Toronto   Sydney

ATRIA BOOKS

1230 Avenue of the Americas
New York, NY 10020

Photo Credits: Unless otherwise credited, all photos are from the author's collection. P. x, courtesy of Brad Hurley; p. 92, courtesy of www.DerekRidgers.com; p. 118, courtesy of Mark Lennihan/AP; p. 142, courtesy of Patrick Hertzog/Getty Images; p. 160, courtesy of People Image; p. 188, courtesy of Krasner/Trebitz; p. 198, courtesy of Todd Oldham; p. 220, courtesy of Scott Bacon.

ISBN-13: 978-0-7432-9187-3
ISBN-10:   0-7432-9187-5

First Atria Books hardcover edition April 2007

1   3   5   7   9   10   8   6   4   2

ATRIA BOOKS is a trademark of Simon & Schuster, Inc.

Manufactured in the United States of America

For information regarding special discounts for bulk purchases, please contact Simon & Schuster Special Sales at 1-800-456-6798 or business@simonandschuster.com.

To Benjamin Lay, "the rebellious gnome"
(1681–1760)

Benjamin Lay, a four-foot-tall hunchback whose
arms were as long as his legs, was so distraught by
slavery and animal cruelty that he shunned city life
and dwelled in a cave near Philadelphia. He made his
own clothes to avoid supporting slave labor and the killing
of animals for their fur or leather, and refused to eat meat
or other animal products. Mr. Lay occasionally ventured into
the city to rant and rave at public meetings about the
hypocrisy of a supposedly religious society embracing such
vicious practices, once thrusting a sword into a hollowed-out
Bible filled with fake blood, which he then sprayed onto the
faces of shocked slave owners. Although considered a pariah
by colonial society, he persuaded Benjamin Franklin to
publish some of his tirades.

Contents

COMMITTED

Chris P. Carrot causes a stir in Des Moines.

Meat Me in St. Louis

The hefty woman at the night desk of the Sleep Inn in Omaha greeted us with maps, brochures, and directions to the ice machine, oblivious to the huge crate we carried past her. She had no idea that it contained the lifeless orange body of a creature, half-man, half-vegetable, whose arrival in Nebraska was receiving the sort of welcome Charles Manson gets at a parole hearing. Safely inside our $39 hideout, we bolted the door, flounced onto the polyester bedspreads, and turned on the late news just in time to see school officials pondering their most challenging task of the semester: how to keep a crusading carrot away from impressionable elementary school students.

"Kids shouldn't talk to strangers," a concerned mother told the reporter, "even if the stranger is a vegetable."

Welcome to the inaugural tour of vegetarian mascot Chris P. Carrot. With my feet in his clunky white shoes, Mr. Carrot stands over seven feet tall, with bright, cartoonlike eyes, a fountain of greenery sprouting from his head, and a wide smile made of dark mesh through which whoever is inside can see out. He holds a poster that reads EAT YOUR VEGGIES—NOT YOUR FRIENDS (we had thought of going with EAT ME but thought again). Completing the ensemble is a pair

2 · *Dan Mathews*

of fluorescent orange panty hose, which, sadly, wouldn't stretch to the top of my lanky legs. I found myself holding the sign with one hand and constantly yanking up the glowing tights with the other.

As PETA's campaigns chief, I don't ask anybody to do anything I wouldn't do myself. Since I cooked up this junket, it was my duty to give the flame-colored mascot a test drive in order to work out the kinks for future carrots. My comrade was recently hired campaigner Tracy Reiman, a chipper gal from Georgia whom I was training. On her first business trip, she had to rise at dawn to help her new boss morph into a reject from the land of H. R. Pufnstuf. Tracy also became the carrot's official spokesperson; the voice I had developed for Chris P. Carrot, a hybrid of John Wayne and Pee Wee Herman, triggered panic-stricken shrieks and projectile tears from second-graders, so we decided on the spot that the carrot should be mute.

Our initial goal was simply to score equal time to tax-funded talks in which the U.S. Department of Agriculture beguiles a captive audience of kids with tales about how meat and milk are produced, using carefree materials such as the "Peace & Plenty Farm" coloring book. It reads:

A farm is like a ball team, and the animals are the star players. They live in buildings so clean they almost squeak. Wouldn't you rather be in a building than outside under a tree on a stormy night?

Students are not informed that the animals are kept in such cramped conditions that factory farmers routinely cut off their horns, slice off their beaks, and grind down their teeth to keep them from mutilating each other. When schools refused our offer of a more realistic classroom presentation, we announced that we'd bring the news to kids just off campus, courtesy of PETA's zany decoy, Chris P. Carrot, whose blazing orange leaflets contained all the grim facts that were omitted from meat-trade handouts. The story exploded throughout Cattle Country.

It was 8 a.m. when we arrived at Fontenelle Elementary School in Omaha, but the frenzied mob made it feel more like an afternoon taping MTV's *Total Request Live* in Times Square. From inside the carrot outfit, all I could hear was the sound of my quickened breath as Tracy led me through the throng of cameras, armed police officers, troubled teachers, angry parents, and the stray disobedient child trying to give me the high five. The only thing missing was a riot squad with fire hoses, and for all we knew, they were hiding in the bushes.

"I'll buy you a Big Mac if you beat it!" a chubby bearded father angrily hollered at me as he snatched the leaflet from his son's hand. The grown-ups' excessive reaction only piqued kids' interest, and they soon engulfed us, cleaning out Tracy's basket of buttons and brochures.

Peering through the carrot's eyehole, I saw myself in the scrutinizing children. As a young carnivore, I never imagined growing up to be an animal rights activist, much less a costumed crusader. I was such a meat enthusiast that my father, Ray, a former chicken truck driver who later opened a diner, named the "Danny Dog" on the kiddie menu in my honor. I savored juicy Reubens, relished the flesh-ripping sensation of biting into a New York strip steak, and scanned the daily specials in hopes of finding a Noah's Ark Platter so that I might sample two of each species. Like many suburban tykes, I held the illusion that meat had nothing much to do with animals, but instead grew in a hamburger patch, as the omnipresent McDonald's ads insisted. Kids love animals so much that many meat companies deceive them with nonsensical commercials, like the one with Charlie the Tuna, the cartoon fish who declares that he tastes so good, he can't wait to get caught and eaten. I scarfed him right down without thinking about it.

That all changed with a ninth-grade punch in the stomach. Although I grew up a fairly gleeful misfit, I was often dragged into traumatizing fights for being gay. One morning, as I rushed down a hallway between classes, one of my critics yelled, "Faggot!" and slugged me in the gut, sending me tumbling over with the wind knocked out of me. Stunned, I looked up to see a collection of chuckling faces as I lay gasping for breath.

A few weeks later, I was on a fishing trip with my dad when my rod bent over like a horseshoe. What could be so heavy? A marlin? A swordfish? *Jaws*? I excitedly reeled in my catch and yanked the pole back, only to discover that all I'd captured was a big, ugly flounder.

"You got a booby prize!" someone joked as he stomped the flailing fish to the deck and tore out the hook, causing blood to pulse from the slimy creature's mouth to the beat of his racing heart. Everybody laughed, but I grew uneasy. I considered what the scene looked like from the flounder's point of view. Stunned, he was looking up to see a collection of chuckling faces as he lay gasping for breath.

In that instant, the flounder was the only creature on board I could relate to. I felt sick. I had become one of the terrorizing bullies I dreaded so much at school. Most people are sensitized to the plight of animals by cute, cuddly, four-legged balls of fur, whereas I sympathized with a rubbery bottom-feeder. I never ate fish again and gradually stopped eating anything else with eyes, except for potatoes.

I eagerly shared my newfound notion of what it meant to be civilized with anyone who would listen, and plenty who wouldn't. Why should "live and let live" only apply to humans? I was naively confident that everybody would grasp this simple, noble logic and adopt the same basic regard for fish and chickens that they had for dogs, cats, and all the other animals with a heart, brain, and nervous system. I might as well have been advocating rights for pet rocks. Although I won a few converts among my teenage punk-rock peers, most people ridiculed me for proposing such a far-fetched idea. This was 1978, when I was fourteen, and from that day on I've been on a mission to promote the very same idea. Thankfully, it's not considered so far-fetched anymore.

For many years I pushed campaigns that appealed to people's intellect and compassion. But as cable TV and the internet helped mold an escapist society hungrier for entertainment than education, serious topics began taking a backseat to scandal and sensation, and we at PETA had to dream up flashier ways to vie for people's attention. Little by little we had to boil the brains out of many of our efforts. But by changing with the tabloid times and using provocative vaudevillian tactics, PETA soon earned a name for itself as one of the most enduring, annoying, and influential pressure groups in the world. Of course, in doing so we often have had to make ourselves look quite silly. Although I lament the loss of serious public discourse, I've easily adjusted to the new rules because I am, at heart, a very silly person.

When I wake up each morning, my first thought isn't *I want to help animals*, but *I want to have fun*. Then responsibility kicks in, and I go to work. But where is it written that just because you have devoted your life to fighting for a serious cause, you can't have a good time doing it? I've known many bighearted people who gave up on the world because they couldn't lighten up. I gallivant all over the globe trying to focus a scandal-obsessed society's attention on the plight of animals, often making a public mockery of myself—and always ready to clock out and get into trouble. I'm a focused person who can't resist a good diversion, and I think that's why I've never burned out, even after twenty-five years on the front lines.

Being a nonconformist, I never imagined that I would have the same job for decades—a job that has entailed being carried off by the police in my underwear at a fur expo in Hong Kong, impersonating a priest to crash a fashion show in Milan, and donning a cow costume to storm a cattleman's convention in Denver. I've conducted business meetings in settings ranging from a skinny-dipping party at the Playboy Mansion to the solemn office of the archbishop of Turin to an ornate box overlooking the Vienna Opera Ball. I've picked up the phone to get an angry earful from Madonna when I spoke out against her bullfighting-themed music videos. I've also picked up the phone to hear Sir Paul McCartney insisting we take the rest of the day off when we'd successfully pressured McDonald's to stop buying meat from slaughterhouses that fail USDA inspection.

It doesn't matter that some people think we're crazy; most kids, whose sense of justice has yet to be corrupted, as mine hadn't been on that fateful fishing trip, absorb the message. This has made animal rights a top concern for today's youngsters, Generation Whatever. In 2006 PETA was named the #1 nonprofit organization that teenagers would volunteer for by a two-to-one margin over the second highest vote getter, the Red Cross. Of course, we don't reach everybody, which brings us back to the midwestern schoolyard escapades of Chris P. Carrot.

After Mr. Carrot's dramatic debut in Nebraska, Tracy and I sped off to Des Moines for the second stop on our Beef Belt tour. The highway was flatter than week-old roadkill, and there was no time for joyriding because a television station had asked to film the carrot as he passed by the city limits sign. If they had known the carrot was gay, I thought, the PTA might have erected a roadblock. Once in Des Moines, to our astonishment, TV crews did live morning remotes from the school cafeteria, interviewing opinionated cooks and sleepy students about what effect the visiting vegetable might have on their lives. But at the school we visited on the afternoon stop, we had some unexpected guests.

The battle cry of our adversaries in Iowa was a simple "Moo!" and their charge was led not with an outstretched sword but with defiant tongs, waving juicy burgers at a counterprotest-cum-barbecue on a dry, patchy, yellow front lawn across the street from the school. A pair of elephantine gentlemen in overalls from the Iowa Pork Producers Association peeled off slices of luncheon meats, handed them to giggling students, and pointed in my direction. It wasn't until a peculiar deli odor started filling my costume that I realized the mystery meats weren't meant to be eaten, but thrown, and even shoved through the Velcro down my back. The dull thuds hitting my orange torso sounded like being in a soft-top car during a hailstorm. Finally Tracy led me away, but a pack of cold-cut-wielding fifth-graders was in hot pursuit, and when we reached our van, it became the kids' new target.

"Fuck PETA, we love meat," they hollered as they pitched pimento loaf at our shiny rental. Using all the self-control I could muster, I said nothing for fear of a fight erupting. One headline we didn't want was CARROT SHOVES BRATS INTO TRAFFIC. We sped away with a piece of bologna stuck to the windshield and our jaws on the floorboard.

"I wish they had thrown something we could eat—I'm starving," I said, desperately trying to put on a brave face for the trainee campaigner as I pulled off my sweaty costume and shook out smelly bits of pig.

Tracy pulled into a small park so we could get some fresh air before we hit the road to Missouri. We sluggishly plopped ourselves down on a bench by the curb, and as my heart rate slowed down to near normal, I felt uncharacteristically despondent. I was rattled by the thought that I had been attacked after class as a teen for being gay, and now as an adult for being a carrot; I guess you could say I've courted hostility for being both a fruit and a vegetable.

Just then, a beat-up beige Plymouth with a bad muffler idled up. The driver, whose hair was twisted into a scraggly gray bun, craned her head out.

"Do y'all know where the Douglas school is? We're looking for the PETA carrot." Was she friend or foe? A bug-eyed child listened intently from the backseat.

"My granddaughter is dying to meet the carrot, but he didn't come to her school," she yelped in a scratchy cigarette voice.

"The carrot went home," Tracy explained as she ambled over to the van to fetch her basket. "But he left you a present." The child leaped out of the car and excitedly grabbed a button, leaflet, and one of the few T-shirts we were able to give out on the entire tour. With our faith in humanity restored, we revved up the engine and pointed ourselves toward Kansas City.

My parents get married; seemed like a good idea at the time.

CHAPTER 1

Atomic Meltdown

The strongest earthquake ever to hit North America struck Alaska on March 27, 1964, killing 117 people and propelling a fifty-foot seismic sea wave southward in the Pacific at 450 miles per hour. Anxious forecasters reported that the tsunami, which battered parts of the Canadian coast, might roar ashore in Southern California overnight.

After watching doomsday predictions on the late news, Ray kissed his wife, Mary Ellen, and went to bed, figuring their small suburban house, located an hour south of Los Angeles near Newport harbor, was on a hill high enough to keep the young family dry. Ray dozed off, but Mary Ellen couldn't. As the town nervously slumbered, she enlivened, feeling the familiar pull of some magnetic force inside that lured her to wherever the action was. Carefully tiptoeing into the bathroom, Mary Ellen combed up her dark blond hair, applied her trademark kissy pink lipstick, slipped out into their maroon Plymouth Belvedere station wagon, and made a beeline for the beach in hopes of beholding history. I was her unwitting accomplice; she was pregnant with me at the time. I was headed for adventure before I was born.

Mary Ellen meandered around closed sections of the Pacific Coast Highway and found a perfect spot near Newport Pier, where she was dazzled by the stars and sea and saluted by fellow disaster fans. Then, without warning, it came. Not the tidal wave, but a radio report that the surge wouldn't amount to much more than a surfable swell. With a sigh, Mary Ellen joined the other disgruntled rubberneckers at a beachfront coffee shop that had stayed open to cater the calamity. She sat alone at the counter, disappointed that Mother Nature had thwarted her late-night sightseeing excursion.

I learned from Mom that life is a parade that is more exciting to march in than just let pass you by. Her independent spirit stems from a ragamuffin childhood spent bouncing between orphanages and foster homes in Virginia and Washington, D.C., where she often skipped school to attend trials at the Supreme Court or watch Congress in action. She was at the Capitol in pigtails when FDR arrived to declare war on Japan.

My parents met in Reno, "The Biggest Little City in the World," in the late 1950s. Mary Ellen had ventured west and become a blackjack dealer at Harold's Club, an old casino with a gigantic mural of stagecoach pioneers that towered above Reno's downtown neon strip. Hired more for her looks than her gaming skills, she dealt cards in shiny cowgirl boots, form-fitting gabardine western slacks, a red-checkered shirt with silver collar tips, a bandana, and a cocked ten-gallon hat. She rented a room by the week at a motel where a handsome, friendly young man named Ray was working for the summer. Tall and trim, with closely cropped dark hair and hazel eyes, Ray had unpretentious charm. One afternoon in the parking lot, while kneeling to fix her hair in the side-view mirror of somebody's jalopy, she spied him approaching.

"Are my bangs straight?" she asked, flashing her baby

blue eyes. They must have been; the two soon got married and moved to Southern California.

Ray, whose Jewish family stowed away on a Canadian-bound boat to flee persecution in the Ukraine in 1902, grew up in a rough Latino section of East Los Angeles. He's a good-humored, hardworking optimist whose passions include the Civil War, road trips, and food, all of which got passed on to me. He often takes bites from everybody else's plates, another trait I inherited. Shortly after my parents married, Dad was employed as a chicken truck driver, but eventually he landed a job managing restaurants, and they settled into a small house in Newport Beach, an upscale town in ultraconservative Orange County. Ray and Mary Ellen, who were active volunteers for John F. Kennedy's presidential campaign, never fit into the prim, atomic-era enclave, but they felt the area was ideal for raising a family. My brother Mike was born in 1963, I surfaced in '64, and Patrick arrived in '67. In keeping with American tradition, my parents divorced in '71.

Having flunked middle class, Mom, Mike, Patrick, and I moved inland to Costa Mesa, a bland suburb made up of strip malls and fast-food joints brimming with tanned white people who were really happy that the weather was nice. We lived in a succession of dingy two-bedroom apartments; Mike got his own room because he was oldest, and Patrick and I grudgingly shared the other room. Mom slept in the living room on a shabby couch surrounded by overflowing bookcases and a thrift-shop television with a wire-hanger antenna.

Although we continually slipped down rungs on the economic ladder, Mary Ellen insisted that we'd always be culturally refined, a declaration she'd make in a dredged-up Southern drawl. Every Saturday morning, as Led Zeppelin blared from a neighbor's apartment, Mom would switch on the classical station and blast opera, live from the New York Met. Then she'd apply a greasy facial and flit about the hovel scrubbing floors and windows, often in tears—not because she hated housework but because she was moved by some emotional aria. Mike, who was always the most sensible among us, shared Mom's tuneful tastes and became a Beethoven buff, often playing his junk-shop violin or the beat-up piano crammed into a corner of the living room. My ears bled. The closest to classical I could get was the Electric Light Orchestra, whose songs I taped off the AM radio when I wasn't giggling with Patrick to a crass Cheech & Chong record. Or cheering in front of the television when my favorite skater flipped an opponent over the guardrail in the Roller Derby. If my brow were any lower, it'd be a chin.

Each evening, when Mom got home from whatever book-keeping job her temp agency had sent her to, Mike, Patrick, or I would have the Hamburger Helper ready, and we'd eat and watch the news. Always up-to-date on local and global affairs, Mom had a sarcastic, unpredictable opinion on everything from bra burning ("What fool with boobs would do that?") to people who tie sweaters around their waist or shoulders ("They should be removed from society"). Once in a while Mary Ellen skipped work to volunteer for an urgent cause of the day, ranging from marching with downtrodden Mexican immigrants to helping Malibu millionaires dig their homes out from under mudslides. She would have nothing to do with the most notable local organization, however: the national head-quarters of the extreme right-wing John Birch Society. Mom readily introduced herself as "the last of the Socialists," which didn't win her invitations to many Tupperware parties.

Most parents shield their children from the world's unrest, which, I believe, has caused an epidemic of apathy;

by the time kids are deemed old enough to "understand," they've grown comfortably accustomed to not caring. Mary Ellen, in her often irrational and always emotional way, made us feel obliged to choose sides in any issue in the news. When Walter Cronkite reported that Anita Bryant was hit in the face with a pie by gays protesting her crusade against Florida's antidiscrimination bill, Mary Ellen leaped from the table and cheered, then turned down the sound to spell out the controversy to Patrick, Mike, and me.

"Gays are boys that love boys and girls that love girls," she said. "Some idiots are threatened by gays because they say the Bible dictates you should only love people in order to have kids, which happens when a boy loves a girl. That's asinine— boys and girls love each other all the time without having babies, and anyway there are too many people in the world." My prepubescent brothers and I didn't really understand the "baby" part, but we loved the idea that somebody tossed pies, and we wanted to meet these pranksters, these gays.

"Boys," Mom continued, "I'm going to enroll you in ballet so you can be around them—they're lots of fun." We were in tights by Christmas, having landed roles as dancing rats in a regional production of *The Nutcracker*.

Mom's political opinions were often shared with politicians, usually by telegram, despite the cost, even if it meant we bounced the rent check. President Nixon received such a telegram, demanding he withdraw troops from Cambodia, and when we didn't receive a favorable reply, an IMPEACH NIXON sign went into our front window.

"Oh, I like Nixon, too," said a simple, smiling neighbor without a trace of irony. "*Merde*," Mom sighed, rolling her eyes. "Well, at least she understood *one* word."

The only filthy phrase in our home was "Mind your own

business." Mom instilled in us a meddling, protective vigilance, which can be traced to the institutional neglect she endured growing up in orphan asylums during the Great Depression. We learned to observe and react to the world around us, to show a sense of responsibility, and to keep an eye out for others. Even animals.

One afternoon during third grade I was walking home from school and spotted some menacing fifth-graders throwing rocks into a bush. I slowed down out of curiosity, though I tried to appear nonchalant, as these were boys who would certainly slug you in the stomach unprovoked. As I strolled by, a miserable screech echoed from the shrub. The boys chuckled. I knelt down to see a terrified, pregnant gray tabby. The cat was trying to hide and had become entangled, looking defenseless and defeated. Our eyes locked, and she seemed to wonder if I, too, was an attacker.

Would these older kids beat me up if I intervened? Unsure of myself, I forced a smile, making them think I might join in the fun while pondering my options. Should I find my brothers or call Mom at work? Should I flag down a cop or knock on the nearest door? The boys had run out of rocks and began chucking sticks and dirt clods at their target, trying to drive her from the bush. What would they do then? I knelt down again, and she looked up at me, full of anguish.

Suddenly oblivious to the junior sadists, I dove under the bush and reached through the low, dry branches to unsnarl the fat cat without squishing her stomach. It wasn't easy; she wailed and tried to claw me, but I managed to pull her free and scoop her up. Without looking back, I dashed across the street and ran home with the squirming bundle, telling her that she was safe and desperately trying to keep calm so I wouldn't call attention to myself in front of the neighbors; our apartment complex didn't allow animals.

Just before dawn the next morning, my disheveled new friend, who I called Duchess, announced her labor with a shriek from inside the closet. Patrick, Mike, and Mom watched from across the room while I lay on my stomach on the shag carpet just outside the half-open closet door to watch the kittens come out. As Duchess dutifully licked the afterbirth off each of her babies, I wondered if she'd devour any of them. "Sick kittens taste like chocolate so the mama cat knows to eat them," a friend had told me. All six were keepers. Oddly, just after the last soggy kitty was out, Duchess gripped her fourth-born by the scruff of his neck with her teeth and, purring wildly, set him down in my hands before positioning herself to nurse the others. He was all white, and I named him Harvey before placing him back down among his siblings. Duchess craned her head to nuzzle my arm and looked at me with pure gratitude. It was a bigger rush than sneaking into an R-rated movie.

Our reputation as the neighborhood "animal people" quickly grew. Not long after we took in Duchess, a kid from across the street knocked on our door to report that a cat was crying on the roof of the school and couldn't get down. Patrick rushed over, climbed up, and brought her home. That was Bridget, another pregnant cat. She needed an emergency Caesarian section that we could ill afford, but somehow did.

Then there were the alley cats who hung out near the smelly Dumpsters behind our building. Some accepted our open invitation to come inside and play, but others kept to themselves, which made us fearful that they'd fall in with the wrong crowd. Like the guy down the block who hurled new-born kittens against a stucco wall like a baseball pitcher practicing his fastball. Or the teens that crushed cats' skulls in the heavy Dumpster lids just for fun. Or the man who strung up fishhooks just inside the torn garage vent to ensnare any cats that might get paw prints on his shiny red car (he and the landlord were at odds over who would replace the vent screen). Yet another danger the felines faced involved our new neighbors: culture-shocked, war-weary refugees from Vietnam who reportedly cooked cats for dinner, just like back home. We learned that life for strays isn't really like Disney's *Aristocats*, so we started a sort of indoor sanctuary. Within months of taking in our first animal, we had a litter in each bedroom closet, plus a few older stragglers, for a grand total of seventeen cats and a dog—in an apartment that didn't allow animals at all.

"I know what it's like to be a stray," Mom told each newcomer with a kiss.

We didn't consider animals pets, but affectionate vagabonds who became members of the family. Although they were lots of fun, we didn't take in animals for our own amusement, but to keep them from the various dangers we'd become aware of. We wouldn't have thought of buying a cat or a dog at a pet shop or even getting one from a shelter, as there were so many four-legged refugees in our neighborhood to tend to. It was a natural extension of our civic-minded outlook.

Although friends from school were envious of our motley menagerie, their parents and most of our neighbors thought we were crazy. Why care about animals when you barely have enough to eat yourself? Instinct, I suppose. Each cat got bathed, spayed or neutered, and a trip to the vet at any sign of illness, even if that meant bouncing a check. We couldn't imagine turning away some bedraggled cat in need of a feline leukemia shot simply because we didn't have the cash.

By the time I was in fourth grade, we had become conscious of every penny, often probing the couch seams for lunch money. Although Dad, who had moved to Florida, was always prompt with child support and alimony and Mom made okay money as a bookkeeper, we had an ever-increasing number of mouths to feed and vet bills to pay. Whenever a knock fell on the front door, we peeped through the bathroom window before answering in case it was the landlord, in which case we'd pretend we weren't home; he was either looking for overdue rent or hoping to witness the Wild Kingdom as grounds for eviction.

Patrick, at six, was too young to work, but Mike and I found odd jobs to help with family finances. For a time I delivered our local paper, the *Daily Pilot*, which we called the *Daily Pile-of-it*. It was invigorating to get up at four, ride around tossing papers from my bike, and be home in time to watch cartoons, get ready for school, and read the paper. My favorite column was the Police Blotter, which reported crimes such as DRUNK TEEN ARRESTED WHILE FIGHTING WITH TREE. Alas, I got canned when the *Pile-of-it* learned I wasn't yet ten years old. Next, I got an afternoon job putting flyers for Gene Ray's Sun-O-Rama tanning salon on car windshields in mall parking lots. That gig was over when South Coast Plaza security stopped me and made me backtrack, taking all the flyers off; I had no idea it was not only an under-the-table job but also unauthorized. I finally found more lasting employment making $25 each weekend at the Swap Meet in the Plant Bus. It was a converted school bus, painted green, which did brisk business selling everything from cactus to wandering Jews. It was run by a friendly hippie who wore tight, grimy blue jeans. During slow times he would occasionally tell me he was horny; I had no idea what he meant, but simply replied, "Cool."

This extra money barely made a dent—we needed to hit a jackpot. Luckily, that's just what happened shortly after my favorite game show, *Joker's Wild,* announced during the closing credits that it would have kids on during the holidays. I was so thunderstruck I nearly choked on a Pringle as I jumped for the phone. The lady who answered at CBS said to write, as instructed on the screen. I hurriedly sent in the required postcard and followed up with pushy calls after school until they told me when the tryout was. Mom took off work, and we giddily drove to L.A. for the cattle-call audition in a busy, sweaty office. I don't remember what they asked; I think they just wanted to make sure the dozen brats they picked from the thousands who applied wouldn't be introverted wallflowers when the cameras came on. Somehow, I passed. This was my first lesson in persistence paying off, and even though it was just a game show, the experience became a big confidence builder for loftier endeavors. With our spirits through the roof, the whole clan got dressed up in our Pick 'n Save finery and went to Coco's Coffee Shop, where Mom bounced a check for a celebration dinner.

For my television debut, in December of 1973, I had long, bushy blond hair and wore an orange velour shirt that zipped halfway down the front and had a big floppy collar. This was accessorized by a polished purple rock dangling from a chain around my neck, a good-luck charm given to me by a friend of Mom's. CBS Television City was thrilling; in the elevator we saw Lee Merriwether with curlers in her hair, getting ready for a *Barnaby Jones* close-up, no doubt, and Dick Shawn, who was in two of our favorite movies, *The Producers* and *It's a Mad, Mad, Mad, Mad World.* On a nearby soundstage, *The Sonny and Cher Comedy Hour* was being filmed, and some of the cast came over to greet us tykes. I was mesmerized by Cher, who seemed like a gracious giant when she leaned over to ask if we liked the salami sandwich tray CBS had provided. I politely nodded, my cheeks bulging like a hamster's with the free grub.

On the show, Mom sat next to me, and my opponent, a pleasant twelve-year-old brunette, sat with her dad. She lost. The only question I got wrong was "Is Chicago's baseball team called the White Sox, Red Sox, or Blue Sox?" If only the sports question had been about Roller Derby. Still, I won; among my prizes were a candle-making kit (loved it), a set of encyclopedias (read 'em obsessively), ten tickets to a hockey game (too bad I didn't have ten friends and didn't care about hockey), a train set (never arrived), and $375 cash with which to buy a college savings bond. As if. That money covered vet bills instead, but Mom surprised me a decade later by giving the money back when I moved to Italy.

Too bad I didn't win a car; our sputtering 1965 Galaxie 500 had entered an automotive black hole, and we couldn't afford to bring it back. Then things turned worse when the landlord told us, "Either the animals go or you go." We went. The problem was how to get there without a car. Fortunately, we found another apartment only a few blocks away.

The evening before we moved, Mom dispatched Mike, Patrick, and me to the Pantry supermarket to snag shopping carts from the lot before they were rolled in for the night. The next morning we began the daylong task of moving all our belongings from Coolidge Avenue to Filmore Way in noisy grocery trolleys. Rattling over sidewalks, we pushed load after load of pots, pans, records, lamps, linens, and, worst of all, heavy books. Mom ignored our pleas and wouldn't throw out even one volume of her hardcover collection of Will Durant history tomes and Agatha Christie novels. Despite stares from our neighbors, she tried to make light of our plight by telling us we were stars in our own sitcom.

"Your friends will never be able to do this," she assured us.

Wheeling around corners was a challenge, but Patrick and I had fun speeding back in the streets with the empty carts. Mike wasn't the least bit amused, however, especially when we had to rumble our already-battered piano over curbs and speed bumps en route to our new abode. Clanging along the cracked sidewalk, the piano played its own artsy sonata, announcing our arrival to our new neighbors, who all came outside to investigate the racket. As the sun set, we clandestinely paraded back and forth many more times, each with a cat concealed under his jacket.

The next Thanksgiving we touched bottom: insufficient funds left us not only without a car, but also without power. Never without a solution, Mom arranged for a restaurant a few stops down the Baker Street line to cook our turkey. On holidays, buses run infrequently, so Patrick and I had a long wait with the heavy broiler pan until the number 32 pulled up. Mike was spared bus duty because he was still reeling from embarrassment at having to ride the raw gift turkey home from Mom's office on his bike, his backpack oozing thawed bird juice; he rarely enjoyed the escapades that can ensue when you are penniless.

No electricity meant a charming candlelight holiday dinner. Customarily, we lit a candle only when somebody died, whether family, friend, or a favorite celebrity. The whole candelabra blazed when Vivian Vance passed. It was one of the few rituals Mom upheld from a Catholic foster parent, along with crossing herself when we drove past roadkill. The glow of the candles made the meal seem more like an eerie Halloween party than a traditional Thanksgiving dinner, which felt right, as we were more *Munsters* than *Waltons*. In any case, we were a family. Mom poured just enough cheap red wine into our 7-Up to turn it pink, and Mike carved the turkey as thankful felines ringed the table for scraps, their silhouettes flickering against the walls.

Nowadays, people often ask how I maintain such a lighthearted outlook in the face of so many dire scenarios in the fight against animal cruelty. I think my upbeat demeanor stems from these destitute days, when no matter how bleak and hopeless life seemed, we still had more fun than anybody else. I think it's an ingrained form of gallows humor. Once, as a cashier in a busy grocery store checkout line was about to announce that our check was no good, Mom whispered to me to pretend I was suddenly ill so that we could rush out, leaving our full cart behind and saving ourselves the embarrassment of being publicly branded deadbeats. I began gagging as if I was about to vomit, with Mom exclaiming, "You poor dear!" as she quickly shepherded me outside, where our feigned anguish turned into genuine laughter. Laughing sure beats crying, though we certainly did some of that, too.

Mom almost never dated, as she wasn't much interested in romance, had no patience for small talk, and didn't really like many people. My father, on the other hand, got rehitched shortly after moving east, to a sunny New Jerseyite named Joan, who debunked any wicked stepmother myth I'd ever heard. To get to know them better, and to satisfy my urge to sample normal middle-class life, I lived with them near Tampa when I was ten.

Mindful of the fact that I'd be living under a roof in which a couple slept in the same bed, Mom discreetly carted me to Colony Kitchen to explain the facts of life. She had already told my older brother Mike, who begged her not to tell me, because, as he said, "Danny will always bring it up when we're trying to eat." I was tingling with excitement over the incredible secret I was about to hear, which Mom said had something to do with eggs. We asked for a corner booth, and in keeping with the mysterious theme I ordered an egg salad sandwich. When the waitress left, Mom leaned over the table to explain how penises and vaginas do business together so that an egg can get fertilized and become a baby. My interest quickly turned to disgust, and I wished I'd ordered something else. Mom quietly elaborated, but hushed up when the waitress brought our order. I reluctantly bit into my sandwich, but couldn't swallow, letting the glob of reproductive foam perch on my tongue. What the hell was I eating? I spit the goo into my napkin, dashed to the bathroom, and rinsed out my mouth. I never did learn exactly how it all works, and forever lost my taste for eggs.

I relished the easygoing year with my dad in Florida. I'd hang out at the Steak & Brew restaurant he managed, eating giant croutons from the salad bar and watching customers sip cocktails and shuffle through the sawdust that decorated the floor while Carole King's *Tapestry* eight-track played. When his shift ended, we sat together. Dad had scotch, Joan had white wine, and I drank Shirley Temples with extra maraschino cherries, although Dad always let me sip real booze. He and Joan both felt that if alcohol was totally forbidden, kids would secretly dive for the bottle. *Cheers.* At home, we often sampled Dad's collection of fruity liqueurs. Once he impressed us by igniting a bowl of apricot brandy, which shattered as he carried it to the table, setting our beige carpet ablaze.

Nagging Dad and Joan to quit smoking was my first pressure campaign. I didn't know or care about it being an unhealthful habit; I was just repelled by the smelly ashes floating about. Sometimes I'd roll up their Salems in the car window to crush them. When they bought more, I'd sway in the backseat and sing in a French accent, "Allouette, put out ze cigaretta, allouetta, because it make me seeck." They eventually stopped.

On Friday nights, Dad took me to synagogue. To please him, I feigned an interest in Judaism and even attended Hebrew school, though I never really felt like I belonged to "the chosen people." One of our first assignments was to write hate letters to Nixon, protesting Egyptian president Anwar Sadat's Middle East peace plan. I felt uncomfortable writing such angry letters about an issue I barely understood. Couldn't we write protest letters to NBC for canceling *Laugh-In*? I dropped out but didn't hang up my yarmulke for good—I went to countless Passover seders and Rosh Hashanah parties, where, luckily, nobody could tell whether I was drinking grape juice or Manischewitz.

My idea of a truly religious experience was bowling. On Saturdays, Joan drove me to junior bowling league, where I sometimes bowled 200 with a sparkly purple ball that matched the necklace that had brought me such good fortune on *Joker's Wild*. I've always found the entire bowling experience enchanting: the cozy lighting, the din of pins violently crashing about, the seedy cocktail lounges, and especially the lovable oddballs who work and play there. One kid in my league taught me to phone the attendant and ask if he had ten-pound balls. "Wear baggy pants and they won't show!" we'd yelp before hanging up.

On Sundays, Dad and I were often up before dawn to go pier fishing in Daytona. Live bait intrigued me. You had to grip the minnow and slide the barbed hook through his gill *just so*, or you could stick him and his heart would race under your thumb and guts could gush all over your hand. It was a real-life game of Operation. Another method involved puncturing the minnow at the ridge of his back and dangling him like a puppet before tossing out the line. Once in the water, when the hooked minnow would pull hard, I would try to imagine what kind of sea monster might be about to chomp down on him. More often than not it was a disappointing mackerel, which we'd throw back. Seeing the trace of minnow on the hook made me feel bad.

At least I haven't killed the mackerels, I reasoned, just ruined their day.

CHAPTER 2

Attaining Outcast Status

It was a bright fall morning when I eagerly sped on my bike to register at Davis Middle School, thrilled at the prospect of making new friends and enrolling in mature-sounding classes like Home Economics and Wood Shop. I was once again living with my mother and brothers in Southern California, and although I was eleven, I felt downright sophisticated, having sampled life on both coasts. Breezing onto the crowded modern campus to lock up my orange Schwinn, I had no inkling how fleeting my gusto to get to junior high would be.

I had always fit the traditional definition of "gay" in that I had high spirits and was always ready to laugh, but kids started calling me a fag because I had a high voice and seemed to laugh for no good reason. I don't mean to imply that I was the class clown, as that would suggest that I amused everyone. It was quite the opposite.

For instance, one day our very earnest middle-aged English teacher read aloud from the paperback edition of that season's blockbuster movie, *Rocky*, in a laudable effort to translate our interest from the screen to the page. Her name was Mrs. Berger, and she wore no makeup but had a tidy

Tween angst.

dark blond bouffant. Walking around the class as she flipped through the pages, she brought to life the final desperate struggle in the ring, assuming the vocal style of both Rocky Balboa and his black boxing opponent, Apollo Creed. It was the funniest thing I had ever witnessed—but nobody else was laughing. I tried to muffle my outbursts, especially when Mrs. Berger and a few students gave me the hairy eyeball, but I wasn't too successful. Finally, at the climax, as she dramatically recited—in perfect ghetto cadence—"'D'ain't gonna be no rematch," I lost all control and was practically convulsing. I received scowls from the students and detention from the teacher. I'm sure this wasn't the first instance in which my classmates muttered "fag" under their breath, but it's the first one that I recall.

Not long after, I arrived late in class one cold morning, all bundled up. Everyone turned around to look at me. Probably out of embarrassment, I felt the need to say something.

"This is a *really* heavy coat," I deadpanned. I then collapsed to the floor, as if crumpling under the weight of a full suit of armor. I thought the dumb antic was mildly comical, but few snickered. Before long, the fag moniker took off full force.

My silly, carefree outlook hadn't bothered kids in grade school, but in junior high I was like a splinter under their fingernails. At first I was ribbed by just a few malicious brats, but others, perhaps wanting to impress the gang, soon joined in. I'd get a shove on the shoulder or a slug in the stomach. Then my bike's spokes were smashed in, and I was the subject of vulgar graffiti. I was physically prodded into fights with other misfits for absolutely no reason other than to entertain a mob. I suppose if I had fought back right away and given a bully a black eye, things might have eased up, but violence simply wasn't something I could appreciate yet.

Junior high is where people begin to assume their social identity in life, and if you happen to attain outcast status, you quickly grow accustomed to seeing the world as an outsider, and it can change you forever. I always had a few close companions but was never welcomed into any circle of friends. As such, I've never felt like I had a peer group, even to this day, even among fellow gays, vegetarians, or Roller Derby enthusiasts. I don't feel higher or lower than anyone, just apart. It's oddly comforting.

My problems at Davis were exacerbated by a series of incapacitating surgeries to correct ingrown toenails, extremely painful procedures that didn't take the first few times; my big toes still look as if they got a massage from the garbage disposal. Not being able to exercise much, I grew fat enough to be called Shamu in swimming class. Worse, I often had to hobble around school in one normal shoe and one clunky, open-toe sandal with my toe wrapped in blood-seeping gauze—not exactly the look that wins you a tween popularity contest.

Naturally, I was the last person picked for sports. The second-to-last person picked was Tony Anderson, who was pegged a pansy by his association with me and because of his obsession with all things Disney. Tony had straight dark brown, shoulder-length hair, and was a pretty boy, despite acne; when he called me "wide load," I'd call him "crater face." We soon became best friends, not just because of our proximity at the bottom of the playground pecking order but because we shared the same offbeat sense of humor. We thrived on the loopy social satire that flourished in the '70s, listening nonstop to Lily Tomlin records after school and never missing an episode of the over-the-top soap opera spoof *Mary Hartman, Mary Hartman.*

Like me, Tony was one of three boys being raised by a single mother, but unfortunately Tony's brothers were handicapped, one with epilepsy and the other with spina bifida. We distracted each other from stress at home and intimidation at school by imagining we were like the alien children in *Escape to Witch Mountain* who simply needed to learn how to use their magical powers for protection against a hostile world. The name of one of the paranormal kids in this movie is Tony, and my new best friend sometimes speculated, late at night at one of our many sleepovers, whether the character might somehow be based on him.

We soon hit the college library, plucking out satanic books containing incantations that we would recite against the worst bullies, though we didn't follow through on all the instructions, as we ruled out animal ingredients, like rat tails and lizard tongues. Why should animals suffer for our black magic? We weren't having much luck with the spells until one Thursday, when we found a particularly eerie curse, which we chanted with intense focus on an unusually hairy eighth-grader who had taunted me with a knife after school. Our imaginations ran wild the next day when he was absent. The whole weekend, we gloated at the prospect of having rid ourselves of a prime pest. On Monday morning, however, our faith in the Dark Arts was shattered when the pest returned to school unscathed.

Gym teachers, who seemed to dislike us as much as the students did, checked attendance by having each kid sit on a yellow dot painted on the blacktop. One day, Tony and I arrived to find that our adversaries had covered our dots in spit, so we sat beside them. Mr. Sweazy, our gruff instructor and also one of my first crushes, told us that we'd be counted absent if we didn't sit on our dots.

"They've been spit all over," Tony complained.

"That's your problem," Sweazy shot back with a smirk.

"Well, if you're gonna mark us absent, we won't need to stay for class," I chimed in. Tony and I happily strode off.

On volleyball day, we weren't so lucky. The teams that got stuck with us told us not to even bother playing, so we just strolled around the blacktop, analyzing our favorite scenes from *Bedknobs and Broomsticks*. Suddenly there was a commotion behind us. Tony turned around, hollered *"Run!"* and sprinted away. I looked around to see four ruffians running toward me, one of them waving the huge net bag used to collect the balls.

"Bag the fag!" shouted Craig, a blond kid with braces.

I pointed myself toward the gym offices but was unable to gain much speed because I couldn't put any pressure on my healing big toe. The kids grabbed me and threw me to the blacktop, pulling the net bag over my head and tying it around my knees. I squirmed on the ground, rolling over a few times, heart pounding and lungs heaving. I tried to sit upright and reach down to untie myself from the inside, but it was futile. My agitators cheered and got much of the class to follow suit. It was like a calf-roping contest at a rodeo. As I staggered to my feet, my face beet-red, I could see Tony fruitlessly pleading with an amused-looking coach.

"Mathews!" the coach ordered. "Collect all the balls!" My rage overtook my humiliation.

"Fuck you!" I screamed in a shrill prepubescent voice as I shimmied the bag off over my head. "This bag is going in the 'shit' locker!"

Tony's jaw dropped. The infamous locker to which I

referred wouldn't latch shut, so kids stuffed it with things like moldy bologna, used tampons, and, yes, shit. I marched away, allowing myself to cry only once my back was to the throng. The bag went into the shit locker, and I got my first suspension from Vice Principal Terry. I trembled as I walked home, wondering if life would always be so hateful, and collapsed in sobs as I hit the couch, where my white cat, Harvey, licked the tears off my cheeks and sat on top of me, purring.

Whenever a story hits the news about bullied kids shooting their classmates, I'm baffled—not that it happens, but that it doesn't happen more often. I cringe at what a busy trigger finger I might have had if Mom had kept guns at home. These experiences gave me insight into the human capacity for cruelty and how easy it is for people to justify violence when they don't understand somebody who is different and thereby judge him to be inferior. All people have a sadistic side—it just bubbles to the surface in some more than others, and worsens when a child is never taught empathy. "Boys will be boys," parents often say. Many kids grow out of it, but the dimmer ones grow up and compensate for low self-esteem by striking out at whomever they can most easily exert power over, whether it's a wife, kids, prisoners, or animals.

Luckily, Tony and I found a safe haven after school in the dusty Costa Mesa Civic Playhouse. It was a ramshackle barn down a dirt road by the fairgrounds that put on exuberant shows with a revolving local cast of *Waiting for Guffman*–like characters. Here, our geeky personalities weren't repellent but appreciated, and we landed leads in several children's musicals directed by a feisty, warm-hearted woman named Patti Tambellini. Patti tied her gray hair into a ponytail and waved her arms dramatically while instructing us on blocking and cues, as if she were conducting the Boston Pops. Handsome Tony was always cast as the hero, and pudgy me as the villain. Among the unsophisticated productions we starred in were *Timblewit, Little Red Riding Hood,* and *Dudley the Docile Dragon,* in which yours truly leaped from the stage in a droopy dragon outfit to frighten the elementary school kids in the Saturday matinee audience. It was my first taste of the lure of a costume's ability to captivate a crowd, and had I not become an animal activist, I may well have become a mascot. Or more likely, a clown.

Rejected from any social life within the confines of school, I soon found a much wider world opening up. With my confidence bolstered by our success at the playhouse, I auditioned for a short USC student film called *Zealot,* about an obsessive medical student who misses her autopsy test, then kills a retarded boy who annoys her at the hospital in order to perform the procedure on him. The director said I was a natural for the role of the retard. Mom told my teachers that I was sick for the two days that it took to film, and she wasn't kidding; I got to zigzag around in a wheelchair and learned to drool on cue. The movie was shot in creepy black-and-white at a disturbing mental hospital where I saw a guy with water on the brain whose head looked like it was about to explode. Other patients giggled, grunted, and groaned from behind the lights; I quietly prayed that they didn't think I stole the role from one of them. During the Q&A at the screening, in a packed USC auditorium, somebody asked the director if she had used a real mentally challenged person for the lead. Mom laughed and nodded her head.

Even with all this exciting extracurricular activity, I badly wanted out of Davis, and so did Tony. Fortunately, our straight A's qualified us to take a test to see if we had enough smarts to skip a grade. The vice principal enthusiastically told us that we both passed, but we joked that he probably just wanted to get rid of us. In any case, we felt liberated and started high school at thirteen.

Tony wasn't such an overt target at Costa Mesa High, but I still got pummeled plenty, mostly because my voice hadn't yet changed, and I was fat. It was especially rough at lunchtime, so we often avoided tormenters by eating across the street at Orange Coast College. Unfortunately, prices at the college snack bar were way out of our reach, so we started shoplifting. Tony was hesitant at first, but soon joined me in appreciating the benefits of a five-finger discount. It was intriguing to see what we could fit up our sleeves, down our pants, or under our coats, like a steamy carton of French fries or even a large Dr Pepper. I could make off with a slice of chocolate cake without so much as smudging the icing. This led to my first run-in with John Law.

One weekend, I convinced Tony that we should graduate from munchies to merchandise. Our mission was to get our hands on every Queen single, so we went to Sears, which had an extensive wall display of 45s. When we thought no one was looking, Tony held a bag open as I piled in records until it was full. Clutching the bulging bag, I led the way to the border between Sears and the mall, dancing a jig as I strode into the free zone like a chubby football player who'd just scored a touchdown. As we gave each other the high five, a young couple appeared out of nowhere and grabbed us by the arms.

"Forget to pay for something?!" the man bellowed.

We'd been nabbed by plainclothes surveillance guards. As they marched us to the security office to call the cops, Tony bawled, but I held myself together with the vain hope that they might not call our parents. When the police arrived, we were handcuffed and paraded through the store for disapproving shoppers to shake their heads at. It was degrading enough to curb our kleptomania, but it also felt kind of glamorous. Tony's mother, Betty, was absolutely livid and forbade Tony from seeing me anymore. But as our pool of friends was pretty much empty, she had little choice but to tolerate me.

In order to become responsible citizens who could actually pay for things, Tony and I forged work permits declaring we were sixteen so that we could work at McDonald's. That greasy gig didn't last long. I'd like to say that I quit in protest of cows being killed for Big Macs—the truth is that we were magically transported to Fantasyland.

It had long been Tony's dream to dance in the Disneyland Christmas parade, and as soon as he got his learner's permit, he polished his tap shoes and counted down the days to the audition. As a total lark, I drove with him to the bustling tryout in Anaheim, just a few towns north of Costa Mesa. After performing some simple jazz moves across the hardwood floor, candidates were diverted to either a "we'll take you" corner or the "you sucked" side. Graceful Tony was immediately accepted. Then it was my turn. I tried to summon up my dancing rat experience from *Nutcracker,* but when I pranced across the studio, I felt more like a hippo in a tutu from *Fantasia.* Tony clapped a hand over his mouth in amazement when the choreographer motioned me to join the takers. Tony was cast as a wooden soldier, while I was concealed inside a giant, shimmering Christmas tree on rollers.

There were eight trees in our little musical forest, four green and four gold, each with cues to flick our lights off and on and spin around to the strains of "Winter Wonderland" in the California heat.

Mom had told me that gays lived in San Francisco, West Hollywood, and New York City, but to my astonishment, Disneyland was where they thrived. Mickey Mouse was played by a short, stocky tractor-tossing lesbian, and Snow White was a tough, bitchy chain-smoker, whose scowl magically transformed into a frozen smile as soon as the gates were flung open. Prince Charming was in fact a queen, and the swishy Disney dancers confirmed my belief in fairies. It was an easy place to come out of the closet, and Tony soon started dating a fellow subject of the Magic Kingdom. By now, I also sensed that I was not just a fag but a homosexual, but because I had been scorned for so long, I couldn't imagine anybody having a romantic interest in me. I was doubly apprehensive because Mom always made fun of anybody who bent themselves out of shape to lure a date.

After work, Tony and I perused the shops on Main Street and squandered our minimum wage earnings on Tinkerbell memorabilia and candy. Since we rarely had enough cash left to eat a proper dinner, we'd ride the elevators at the Disneyland Hotel, stop at each floor, and see if any leftovers had been set out in the halls on room service trays. We called this form of dining "crackering," as Saltines were sometimes all the pickin's that remained. It wasn't unusual to find a few sips of wine, or to yank away the cloth napkin to reveal half of a cold pepperoni pizza. We occasionally crackered at other hotels, but the offerings at the crowded Disney resort were always the best.

· · ·

With our expanding horizons, Tony and I were among a slightly older crowd, and our theatrical interest matured from community theater and parades to the *Rocky Horror Picture Show,* which had recently begun showing at midnight. Tony liked to go once in a while, but I had to go every single weekend, and finding a ride to *Rocky Horror* became my constant obsession.

One new friend with wheels who was eager to participate was Theresa Cordano, an upbeat Italian I had met in drama class. As neither of us was yet old enough to get into an R-rated movie without our parents, Theresa and I found that an easy way to get past the doorman was to dress in costume. Theresa would come over on Saturday nights at ten o'clock with her cosmetics bag, and we'd start glopping on Glam Rock makeup. We were often the most outrageously dressed Time Warpers, and the theater started letting us in for free, and soon offered us $20 each to do a floor show before the movie. Theresa and I often performed as the Brad and Janet characters, though I sometimes came as Meatloaf's biker character, Eddie, and clumsily rolled down the aisle on a motorcycle supplied by the theater. It was absolutely terrifying.

Theresa's seventeenth birthday was a greatly anticipated occasion because it meant that we'd be able to legally get into not just *Rocky Horror* but other dirty and scary movies. The big day came on Good Friday, the thirteenth of April, 1979, and we made plans to celebrate at Farrell's Ice Cream Parlor. That night, driving her VW bug, Theresa picked me up first, wearing a red, white, and blue birthday hat. We then stopped to cram in a few others, including Theresa's best friend Margaret, who brought the cake. Suddenly, as we drove down a quiet side street, with the Cars' "Good Times Roll" blaring from Theresa's cheap speakers, everything faded to black.

In the strange void, screams and the sound of crunching metal swirled around me. I felt as if I was falling in complete darkness and wasn't sure I had legs anymore. We had slammed into a parked car, and I was thrown forward from the backseat, knocking out the front windshield with my forehead, and remained unconscious for nearly an hour. Because a VW's engine is in the back rather than the front, the metal carry-all rack installed below the dashboard squished into Theresa's guts full force, sending her seat off the track and onto my legs.

When I came to, everybody had been taken out of the car except me and Theresa, who lay still in her seat on top of me, a trace of blood dripping from her mouth. Her birthday hat was crumpled beside me, and blood-spattered cake smeared the floor where Margaret had been. My legs hurt so bad I wanted to wail, but I was too bewildered. A husky fireman leaned into the car.

"What's your name, son?"

I didn't know.

"What year is it?" he continued.

"Huh?"

I was in a daze and realized that we'd been in an accident only when they gently slid Theresa from her seat, then pulled me through the passenger door. As police lights whirled, I was hoisted into an ambulance, where Margaret was laid out on a stretcher. She looked at the huge knot on my head and quipped, "Looks like you got your Easter egg."

We had a funeral for Theresa instead of a birthday party. I'd never known of anyone who died on the day they were born, much less on Friday the thirteenth. Her open casket service was the week after Easter, and those of us in the accident came bandaged and bruised. Theresa's heartbroken parents, who were charismatic Catholics, smiled joyously as they told me that God loved her so much that he called her home early. In a postconcussion stupor, I kissed Theresa's cold, clammy cheek and slipped her *Rocky Horror* fishnets into the coffin.

After tasting the glory of the holiday parade, Tony took the necessary tests to leave high school and follow his dream from Disneyland to Disney World, where he had secured a role in the magnificent Main Street Electrical Parade. I would miss him at school, but I totally supported his decision. He was a year older than me, and I began to see Tony as a young adult embarking on an exciting life after a very troubled adolescence. As Tony prepared for the big move to Orlando, we had a farewell lunch in Frontierland on the open-air patio of the Hungry Bear restaurant, overlooking the fake Mississippi River near the Haunted Mansion. We bragged about being the first of our school to take on the real world and became giddy thinking about the adventures that lay ahead. As we grazed on French fries, I had no inkling how final a farewell it would be. As often happens with childhood friends, we lost touch.

Over a decade after Tony and I had last spoken, his brother Jeff nearly fell out of his wheelchair when he saw me on *Jerry Springer* debating leaders of a religious cult that sacrifices animals. That evening, their mother, Betty, left a brief message on my voice mail at PETA asking me to call. Although she sounded cheery, the fact that she didn't mention Tony somehow confirmed my long-held worry that since Tony had come out well before safe-sex guidelines were established, he had contracted AIDS. Sure enough, Betty delivered the dreaded news of his untimely death. The world seemed to stop spinning for a moment. Tony had tried to find me as he wasted away, she explained, but it wasn't to be. She broke the awkward silence by saying that one of Tony's dying wishes was for me to scatter his ashes around the Peter Pan statue in London. I made arrangements to see her the very next week.

"I always thought you were such a terrible influence on Tony, and here I am handing you his remains," Betty said in the parking lot of the car dealership where she worked, as she passed me a brown Tupperware-like container that rattled like a maraca when I shook it. Her words, the heat, the haze, and the new and used cars surrounding us would be forever imprinted in my mind.

I didn't declare Tony on my landing card while flying to England, as I was afraid they might not let him in. When the customs clerk at Heathrow asked what was in the tub, I quickly opened the lid to hide the funeral parlor sticker, ran my fingers through the charred bone fragments, smiled, and said, "Potpourri." A friend in London later told me that I should have simply declared Tony as a "duty-free spirit."

The next day, in the early morning fog, I strode through Lancaster Gate into Kensington Gardens and over to the Peter Pan statue to sprinkle the pixie dust that had once been Tony Anderson. He was off to Neverland, where, as Sir James Barrie wrote in 1911, you never grow up.

Connie Pearson.

CHAPTER 3

"Dan Mathews: We Will Kill You"

Unlike just about every other teenager living near the beach, Connie Pearson's milky skin was never tanned. She had short, vivid red hair, which was always subject to change color, and wore faded Eisenhower-era party dresses. Despite her startling appearance, Connie's demeanor was one of calm, unemotional intelligence. She was clearly very perceptive but gave the impression of being aloof, a combination of traits I found fascinating. I had admired her from afar at school, where, like me, she didn't belong to any clique and was often alone, but seemed engaged in a more vibrant world off campus. Connie was the first punk rocker at Costa Mesa High.

Fate brought us together one afternoon on a bus to Hollywood to watch a taping of *Fernwood Tonight*. This TV series was a parody of small-town talk shows hosted by Martin Mull and Fred Willard, with guests such as a Shirley Temple lookalike who tap-danced on an iron lung while the man stretched out inside played her piano accompaniment. Connie was with her friend Nathalie and I was with Tony in the seat behind them. By the time the bus made its forty-five-minute journey, I had befriended the most influential person I'd ever meet.

Although Connie is the quiet type, we found plenty to talk about, such as our enthusiasm for thrift shops. But whereas I just appreciated finding cheap clothes, Connie was fascinated by trinkets from the escapist culture of the 1950s, such as vintage *Life* magazines, oblong aqua-colored dinner plates, and records by bongo players or Lawrence Welk, who shared space in her musical pantheon alongside newer phenomena like the Sex Pistols and the Bags. Connie was also captivated by Disney, and she widened her eyes in disbelief when I told her that I had just finished a stint as a tree in the Christmas parade. We soon moved on from talking about the things we loved to what we hated—just about everything to do with modern-day culture.

"That's what punk is about," she explained. "If you don't like society as it is, create your own."

I eagerly accepted Connie's invitation to see her band, Soviet Life, a short-lived group that played shows in parking lots, parties, or wherever they could. At the time, few clubs would book this new breed of bands, which was not yet much of a niche market. I saw Connie play at an all-night Laundromat for a crowd of about twenty. It was a bizarre bunch; the shorter ones merrily played in the jumbo dryers, and everyone seemed gleefully broken off from the real world. Some of them scared me a bit at first; the guys looked intimidating in their ripped shirts and spiked hair, and the girls were pale, with thick eyeliner ringing their eyes like raccoons, nothing like the bronzed surfers with feathered hair and designer jeans who roamed the halls at school. Even more shocking was watching Connie's detached demeanor transformed into focused fury when she screeched into the microphone. It was like a primal scream, and although nobody could understand the words, the rage was unmistakable.

A few weeks later, Connie invited me to a ratty bar across town called the Cuckoo's Nest to see an all-girl punk band from Hollywood. I had never been to a nightclub, but my forged work permit convinced the doorman to let me in as long as I didn't attempt to drink. The beer-swilling crowd gravitated toward the ramshackle platform in the corner as the skinhead chicks climbed onstage to blast twangy surf rock. It was an early, rousing gig by the Go-Go's, years before they renovated themselves into pop superstars (and PETA's first pinups). One frenzied song had a chorus that asked, "How much more can I take before I go crazy?" This musical sentiment summed up my little world much more accurately than "Love Will Keep Us Together," and I felt like I had found my long-lost tribe.

Although punk had already exploded in London and had taken root in New York and Los Angeles, it was still novel—and extremely threatening—in conservative Orange County. The cynical, angry lyrics reflected how I had long felt about the artificiality of mainstream society and the kids who taunted me at school. The quirkiness that had long been my social liability endeared me to my new punk friends, and I was instantly attracted to the scene's frantic energy and shocking do-it-yourself fashions. Now I could revel in my role as the outcast instead of just being a victim.

Connie became my antistylist, replacing my bland Kmart fashions with clownish duds from Goodwill and pegging my flared pants with safety pins. Using a razor blade, she hacked away at my wavy locks until I looked like I had been prepped for brain surgery. Worried that I didn't look sufficiently psychotic, I gave myself a bleach job. Unaware there was such a thing as *hair* bleach, I pressed my eyelids closed and carefully poured Clorox over my head in the musty laundry room behind our apartment complex. My hair turned the color of a freshly charged car cigarette lighter.

The next week I sat in class with orange scarecrow hair and minor chemical burns, peeling scarlet scabs from my scalp and artlessly collecting them in the pencil groove at the top of my desk. I leered at my dumbstruck, suddenly wary peers. Any embarrassment I felt was replaced with an unsound sense of empowerment as I returned each bully's baffled gaze with a demented grin. I was shedding the skin of the pathetic punching bag to reveal the amused alien that lurked underneath.

Before punk, I was recognized as a misfit only at school; afterward it was wherever I ventured. The roar of disapproval came with more hostility than I could have imagined—not just from riled-up students, who threw the expected profane barbs and punches between classes, but even the local police, who suddenly swerved to give the new village idiot jaywalking tickets. Almost all of my teachers became anxious, and portly Principal Packer even phoned my mom to say that I might be expelled if I didn't grow my hair longer and fit in with the others. She laughed and reminded him that just a decade earlier, in the 1960s, students were threatened if they had long hair, and said that as long as my grades were good, I could wear wigs to class if I wanted.

Because she was a girl, it was almost acceptable for Connie—and our other new punk friends Mary, Sharron, Nathalie, Laurel, and Julie—to help introduce this peculiar new style to our conventional little town. But for some reason, as the first punk guy, I was looked upon as the Antichrist; I may as well have painted a giant target on my giant body. Kids lobbed food at me during lunch, hollered at me in the halls, and thwacked me on the back of the head in class. I wrote an editorial for the school paper decrying the unprovoked attacks, but it didn't do any good.

At last, I fought back. One lunch hour a steel sprinkler head was thrown at me from a group of hecklers, thwacking my wrist and drawing blood. Finally feeling pushed over the edge, I didn't just look the other way, but returned fire. Though I've never been very physically coordinated, I somehow nailed my assailant in the temple with the sprinkler head. A mini geyser of blood pulsed from his forehead. Within seconds his face was covered in blood. He lunged at me, and we rolled around on the ground. A huge crowd gathered, and word swept through it that my opponent's face was seeped in blood because I had scraped the pavement with it. Soon I was in the middle of a frightening free-for-all in which I was swept away like the Frankenstein monster to the principal's office. I was slapped with a weeklong suspension. The next morning the school entrance was spray-painted with the message, "Dan Mathews—we will kill you." Odd as it may seem, upon hearing the news of the graffiti over the phone at home while watching *The Price Is Right*, I felt like I had arrived.

The press started covering the budding punk scene as an ominous plague encroaching on the peaceful suburbs. After school one day, a *Los Angeles Times* reporter approached me for an interview. Unsure if she was really a reporter or what the angle might be, I nervously joked that I simply dyed my hair and wore shredded Salvation Army clothes for fun and that I preferred show tunes to the Sex Pistols, only to be embarrassed when the quote made it into print as part of a front-page story entitled PUNK'S MENACING PROFILE. Around the same time, a photographer from the *Long Beach Press-*

Telegram shot Connie and me and a few other unsettling characters around the pool table at the Cuckoo's Nest. Yellow-haired Connie was wearing a white button-down dress shirt onto which she had smeared excess purple hair dye, and I sported a striped referee's shirt with a big skull and crossbones pinned on, my now blue-black hair spiked with Vaseline. The headline above our photo was RADICALS FROM RICH HOMES. The writer, whom we had never met, had concluded that Orange County punks were just upper-middle-class brats bored with 1970s styles. Although this was the case with some kids, most of us—certainly all of us in the picture—were just white trash with colored hair.

"Don't complain," Mom said, laughing. "It's the only time in your life you'll be called rich."

Though many kids were hostile, a few curious individuals wanted to know where the action was in this new underground scene. If they had a car, I befriended them in order to snag a ride to Hollywood to watch bands like X, who did a catchy number called "Nausea," and the Dead Kennedys, whose debut album was titled *Fresh Fruit for Rotting Vegetables*. Then there were the Germs, whose sloppy, poetic singer Darby Crash sang, "If I'm an animal I can do wrong, but they say I'm something better, so I've got to hold on." I saw their breathtaking show at the Starwood four days before Darby overdosed on heroin.

Often, the unsuspecting civilian I persuaded to drive to these hardcore freak fests would become alarmed by the Halloween-like crowd—or by the riot squads that often congregated near the clubs—and scram, leaving me to cast about for Orange County punks willing to drop me off in Costa Mesa. On these nights out, I usually told my mom I was just going to a party so that she wouldn't worry that her fifteen-year-old was hitchhiking forty miles from Hollywood on a school night.

In 1980, when it was announced that Siouxsie and the Banshees would come from London to play their first American shows, Connie and I couldn't stop listening to their gloomy masterpiece, *Kaleidoscope*. The lyrics of the frantic closing song, "Skin," jumped out at us: "Mink, seal and ermine, smother fat women. I have a noble cause for skin—there's just too many of them. Cover me with skin, for dancing in!" The song mocked fur wearers, and we cheered when the moody band performed it live at the Whisky A Go-Go. Like me, Connie was crazy about cats, and "Skin" got us thinking about other animals. To us, fur seemed like a dusty prop on an old TV show. The idea of killing minks for fashion seemed as mindless as killing fish for fun. Because my concern for animals was often scoffed at, I felt a sense of vindication and empowerment when trendy Siouxsie addressed the issue in such a wonderfully sarcastic song.

Connie's bashful mother, Mary, a devout Christian Scientist who rarely left the house and never seemed to change out of her housecoat, was always distraught over our flamboyant clothes and taste in music but told us that "Skin" was the first song we ever blared that made any sense. Mary was a member of some animal protection organization. She showed us the latest newsletter, which announced an upcoming protest against Siberian tiger hunting at a foreign consulate in Westwood. Connie's equally demure dad, Chester, offered to drive us all there after his weekend lawn-mowing ritual. As punks, we loathed the idea of ever being seen anywhere with our families, but this trek seemed meaningful. It was an odd troupe; Ward and June Cleaver up front with a juvenile Sid and Nancy in the back. There wasn't much small talk, as Connie and I couldn't stop laughing to ourselves over a huge blade of grass lodged in her dad's black horn-rimmed glasses as he obliviously drove the clunky old car.

My first demonstration was far from an exhilarating, life-changing experience. Aside from our feeble carload, the only participants were a blind woman in a wheelchair with an illegible picket sign propped against her knees, and her nurse. Beachgoers whizzing by in their convertibles probably thought we were waiting for one of those handicapped assistance vans to take us back to the home. There wasn't much of a sense of revolution. Connie and I lasted about ten minutes before she wrestled the car keys from her dad so we could visit the punk shop Poseur, and buy more hair dye.

Undaunted, Connie went through the Yellow Pages and called every other animal-related group to see if more exciting crusades might be in the works. Most listings were for grooming services and pet supplies, but among them was a tiny entry with just three words: Society Against Vivisection. A craggy voice answered SAV's phone; it belonged to an ex-biker named Judy Striker who said she was helping plan an action against an animal experimenter who was being feted by psychologists at the Anaheim Convention Center. He had recently been busted for performing grisly nerve tests on monkeys. We were intrigued, and promised we'd be there.

It was a cloudy day outside the American Psychological Association's annual meeting. The APA's featured speaker was Edward Taub, a man who severed nerves in monkeys' limbs, then used pliers and a cigarette lighter to see if he could get the animals to register pain in their floppy arms or legs. Taub kept one monkey's severed hand on his desk as a paperweight. The procedures and animal care were so sloppy that his Washington, D.C., lab had been raided by police following an undercover investigation by a brand-new group called People for the Ethical Treatment of Animals. PETA's young founders Ingrid Newkirk and Alex Pacheco led the Anaheim rally, which was made up of middle-aged housewives, an angry pack of seniors, Judy, Connie, and me. We held signs but felt silly chanting—it seemed so old-fashioned, so "hippie."

As delegates arrived for the convention, security guards began pushing us away from the entrance. Ironically, it wasn't the young punks or the ex-biker who resisted, but a gaggle of enraged grannies; they encircled the white-coated effigy of Dr. Taub, lit it on fire, and chanted, "Burn Slow! Burn Slow!" It was like a riot at a retirement home, a thrilling spectacle, the likes of which I've not seen since. More important, it made the news, which meant thousands of people would be aware of this mad doctor's dirty work, and groups like the APA might think twice about inviting such a disgraceful speaker.

After the protest, as the cloudy skies gave way to rain, Connie and I excitedly drove to Del Taco to sip Tab and ponder our new role as animal activists. PETA's case against Dr. Taub had made us very curious about the secretive, widespread world of animal experimentation. The idea of a live animal being pinned down and mutilated made me shudder, and I couldn't imagine anyone, especially an educated person, causing such suffering. We then peeled apart some of the soggy research protocols handed out at the demo; beagles were choked in smog labs, rabbits were blinded by cosmetics companies, dogs had their veins crudely clamped in heart studies, and baby monkeys were used in maternal deprivation tests. In these experiments, infant monkeys were pried from their mothers and placed in a cage with nothing but a metal pole, which they pathetically hugged, as it was all they had. Government researchers then pushed buttons to make the pole burning hot and even eject spikes to see how much abuse an infant might take while still clinging to what he sensed was his mother.

I didn't need to be convinced that the tests were frivolous; I would have been against them regardless—just as I was against the Nazi experiments on retarded children and Jewish prisoners I had learned about in Hebrew school, despite Dr. Mengele's excuse of scientific curiosity. I think any civilized person who finds the courage to learn precisely what is done to animals in labs or to watch the footage can't help but feel the same. Sadly, most people can't bear the excruciating details and tune out the cruelty, allowing it to flourish away from public view.

When animal tests make the news, it's often just a vague phrase uttered in connection with a promising wonder drug or procedure that never seems to materialize. In the '70s, the big news was that saccharine caused cancer in lab rats, which was considered a lifesaving breakthrough until people learned that the study was funded by the sugar trade in an attempt to scare consumers away from the competition. The same charade happens year after year in different guises, but few people glance past the headline or blurb to learn what scurrilous drug company or other vested interest lurks behind each carefully crafted and scientifically suspicious animal test.

Some of the other brochures Connie spread out on our table at Del Taco dealt with an issue I was much more reluctant to rally behind: vegetarianism. Although I had stopped eating fish after seeing firsthand how they struggle and suffocate, learning about intensive factory farming was too much for me to digest, so to speak. For people with a conscience, education comes with responsibility, and I was already feeling overburdened. I may have been young, but I already had habits I couldn't imagine changing, such as a delicious diet of barbeque ribs, chicken pot pie, and the mystery meats doled out in the cafeteria. I did, however, avoid organ meat, especially liver, as I had learned in biology class that the liver is the organ that filters out the gunk that your body can't process. Why would anyone want to put refuse like that in their mouth? For Connie, becoming a complete vegetarian was simple, and she did it almost immediately after studying up on the issues.

Since I wouldn't read the literature, she insisted we go to a film festival in Century City for the American premiere of a British documentary called *The Animals Film*. It had just been a major sensation in England, where it aired on Channel Four in a daring bit of prime-time programming that helped sensitize the whole country. One of our favorite bands, the Plugz, was playing just outside the screening, which made the excursion seem fun, so I agreed to go. The well-dressed crowd was a mix of animal protectionists and the film buffs who attended all festival functions. Connie and I enjoyed studying the many plastic surgery disasters that often litter such glitzy affairs.

The Talking Heads provided the song "I Need Something to Change Your Mind" for the opening sequence, in which black-and-white newsreel footage shows a range of cruelties from decades past, including the electrocution of an elephant to demonstrate the power of electricity. The film then goes on to reveal the basic day-to-day life in the parallel world that exists alongside modern humanity, the one most people rarely think about, the animal world. In a very dry manner, the documentary shows how countless cats and dogs are put down in shelters because people don't fix their animals, how minks and foxes frantically pace their cages on fur farms before being electrocuted for their coats, and how researchers at a well-funded whim, blind, scald, and dismember almost every species.

I looked around the crowded theater and was instantly reminded of the scene in *A Clockwork Orange* in which Malcolm McDowell's thug character is strapped into a chair with his eyes clipped open and forced to watch violent images in an effort to get him to change his ways. Some people dashed out in tears, while most of the rest of us quietly sobbed in our seats. I was shaken, but because I had been involved in animal protection since childhood, having dealt with issues such as dog and cat overpopulation and more recently fur and experimentation, I felt a smug sense of superiority. Until the factory farming segment began.

First, we met the docile cows, who are painfully branded, dehorned, and castrated as they begin their journey to become hamburgers. Then came the screaming sows being chained to the "rape rack" while a dutiful pig farmer leads a frenzied boar in to impregnate his stock, all of whom ultimately end up hoisted by a hoof to have their throats slit, their legs flailing violently, with guts and feces spilling like candy from a piñata onto the floor amid gushes of blood.

Next came the chickens. Noisy footage of the birthday process at an egg-laying farm showed the unusable males being tossed like big squirming cotton balls into a trash bin; those who don't suffocate are killed by the shredder. The females have their faces pushed into a hot guillotine, in which their beaks are seared off to prevent them from pecking each other to death in their cramped cages. A close-up showed one disoriented chick with blood dripping onto her fuzzy yellow chest; her face was shoved too far into the machine, and her tongue got burned off along with her beak. Shortly before becoming McNuggets, the chickens have their legs clamped into a rooftop conveyor belt. They bounce down the line, shrieking like little withered old men, straining to swing their heads away from the spinning blade that slices a giant gash in their necks; some bleed to death, others are dumped live into a tank of scalding water for defeathering.

As the devastating epic ended, with a scene showing joyous kids playing among the smiling hamburger puppets in a McDonald's Playland "hamburger patch," I leaned over to Connie and said, "You win." I wish documentaries like *The Animals Film* were shown in high schools alongside USDA-produced cartoons so that kids could get a more factual education and make informed choices about what they eat. I picked New Year's Eve of 1981 as the last day I would eat meat, figuring I'd gorge myself on it for a few months so that I'd really be sick of it for life. My last hamburger was at Bob's Big Boy, and it was a real strain to ingest it before my friends and I hit a garage party to join in the slurred countdown to midnight.

Although I had always been an agitator by nature, it was only when I became a total vegetarian that my antisocial skills felt reconciled. I figured that whatever violence I'd encountered for being "different" paled in comparison to what was happening to animals, and I became so strident that people were uncomfortable having meals with me. My dad and Joan, who by this time had moved to California and ran a diner east of Los Angeles where I occasionally bused tables on weekends, had to deal with my plastering antimeat stickers on the menu. Dad, who hoped that punk was just a passing phase for me, was dumbstruck at the new direction my disruptive behavior was taking. I had inadvertently become a rebel with a cause. Aside from a few friends and my mom, who soon became vegetarian, nobody wanted to hear hideous farming facts or see slaughterhouse photos. They deflected the issue just as I had only months before, saying they already had enough turmoil to deal with in life. I was too young to know that apathy and indifference are more easily conquered with charm than antagonism, a simple strategy that took me years to refine.

It's easy to see why vegetarians often ghettoize themselves like immigrants, millionaires, truckers, or any other put-upon minority; by hanging out with compatible people, you avoid countless daily frustrations. But I'm averse to separatism, a sentiment I first felt as a skeptical brat in synagogue. I've never liked to surround myself with too many like-minded people: it makes life boring and takes away the thrill of evolving somehow from a contrary influence. Maybe the constant challenge keeps me from getting lazy.

While I was busy arguing publicly with people about animal rights, Connie, unbeknownst to me, went quietly underground and got involved with the Animal Liberation Front, the clandestine group that breaks into labs to free animals. She worked on one of the ALF's first big raids in the United States, at the City of Hope in the San Gabriel Valley. Connie doesn't mind me revealing her involvement now, as the statute of limitations on that invasion has long since passed.

This action, prompted by an inside whistleblower, involved getting more than a hundred animals out in trucks in the middle of the night, so the group set up twenty-four-hour surveillance for two months. Connie volunteered for the graveyard watch, driving out from Hollywood at midnight in a skimpy black dress after her shift ended at the Mikado, a seedy club where she was paid 27 cents a minute to dance with mostly Asian businessmen. The nights outside

City of Hope were excruciatingly long: she couldn't read because she had to observe everything, and the light might have attracted unwanted attention from security.

Her spy work paid off when America got one of its first uncensored looks inside an animal laboratory. The ALF filmed their raid and released videos showing dogs, rabbits, cats, and mice disfigured in various medical experiments. The group also removed files that showed many animals had died of neglect before tests were even completed. Amazingly, the government responded by fining City of Hope.

At sixteen, I graduated from Costa Mesa High, but not without a few more silly dramas. As a joke, the student body voted me homecoming prince for the senior prom, at which I was to take the stage with a homecoming princess. My princess was so horrified at the prospect of being paired with me that her parents and the faculty intervened and had me officially disqualified, even though I never had sought to participate and never would have attended. I thought this humiliating shenanigan was very funny.

Less funny was what happened at graduation. I refused to stand for the Pledge of Allegiance, partly because I've always been uncomfortable with nationalism and partly because I didn't want my farewell from high school to be an insincere solemn moment with people I'd always detested. As I sat in silence on the bench, in a sea of green robes, someone angrily kicked me in the head from behind, sending my tassled cap flying toward the football field and many of the students into fits of laughter. I didn't even look around to see who it was. I just tried to keep mindful of one thing: I would soon be very, very far away from Orange County.

At home among the ruins.

CHAPTER 4

Young Hustler, Ancient Rome

If you are lucky enough to travel when you're young, everything you see becomes a part of you on which you can draw all through life.

—ALFRED HITCHCOCK

Although my family tree's roots are in Russia, the distant land I feel most connected to is Italy. It's not the Renaissance palaces of Florence, the fashion in Milan, nor the art or churches that enchant me, but gritty ancient Rome and all points south, like Naples and Sicily, destinations tourists usually find too grubby and chaotic. I've always been captivated by the ancient world and its ruins, no matter how dilapidated. I was sleepy and seventeen when my train trudged past the remnants of the two-thousand-year-old aqueduct and into Rome's smelly Termini station, where I disembarked with the sense of a long-overdue homecoming, rather than an arrival in a strange city where I didn't even speak the language.

Like many teenagers pondering what the hell to do with their lives, I had become morbidly depressed, so I decided to start life anew in a place where I didn't know anybody. I think you get a better sense of who you really are and what you want from life if you move far away from home as soon as possible, at least for a few years. The world offers infinite possibilities, but many are oblivious to them. Even the most agreeable families, as mine was, have expectations that can influence you into falling for an ill-fitting career, spouse, or lifestyle—which leads lots of folks directly to a midlife crisis. I wanted totally new surroundings: not just a new city, but a new country, language, and culture to rejuvenate my dispirited mind and inspire me to figure out my schtick in life.

Since I felt so out of place in the world's newest metropolis, I figured I'd try living in one of the oldest, so I saved up $1,000 waiting tables and fled Los Angeles for Rome to study history. It had always been my favorite subject, but the limited amount of world history taught in American schools left me with more questions than answers. People often asked what I planned to do professionally with a history degree; I never aimed to teach. I was just curious to learn how humanity developed into such a big mess so I might discern how to best push for progress. Ultimately, I wanted to work to change the way people thought about and treated animals, but first I wanted to learn how past movements had motivated the apathetic masses.

I was especially fascinated by the strategies early Roman church leaders used in the fourth century to lure the throngs from paganism to Christianity; to a large degree, this involved partying. As it became clear that the ancients wouldn't abandon their centuries-old blowout to celebrate the winter solstice, when they worshipped sun deities to herald the coming of longer days and a new year, shrewd promoters of Jesus started proclaiming that His birthday happened to fall on that same week, thereby allowing the kegs to keep flowing but with a new Christmas theme. It took a few hundred years, but eventually they had the revelers praying to the son of God rather than the god of the sun. A few thousand years later, after the industrial revolution, when money began displacing mysticism as the public's major obsession, business leaders revised the holiday once more, so that it focused on buying gifts for people, especially kids, who soon became more concerned about what the colorful new Santa Claus icon might bring than the principles of some sad, scruffy guy on a cross. It's easy to be a prisoner to the limited outlook of your era, but learning what has prompted society to evolve (or mutate) can offer insight and patience to those trying to modify antiquated customs, whether they're promoting women in politics, blacks in business, gay marriage, or a vegetarian diet.

I studied near Piazza San Silvestro at a friendly hole-in-the-wall university, for which my dad paid $1,500 tuition, and lived in a bland modern building that housed a lot of students. Among them were Liliana, from Yugoslavia, who would read your fortune in the grounds of your overturned espresso cup; Patrizia, a deranged-looking beauty from Ancona who dabbled in heroin and clothing design; and a pair of sisters from Syria nicknamed "Good Seed" and "Bad Seed" for their very distinct personalities. There were also young Americans, many of whom seemed to be on more of a shopping-abroad than study-abroad program. One student who everyone refused to bunk with was Michael Filippis, a flamboyantly frank Italian-American homosexual from Connecticut. Since I was on a cut-rate program, paying a fraction of what the other students were, the university assigned Michael to be my roommate and told me I had no say in the matter.

"Oooh, your hair is lemony!" he squealed when we met, referring to my latest hair color. I dreaded him at first, but Michael and I soon clicked for the same reason I clicked with many of the friends I made as a teenager: because few others could stomach us. Michael was plump and tan, with wavy dark blond hair and pale blue eyes. He squinted in the sun but shunned shades, explaining, "I don't want to hide my best feature." Actually, his best feature was his devious wit. The first thing he did in our apartment was to invite over the most uptight students, including many of those who refused to room with him, and have them gather at the foot of the stairs. When they had anxiously assembled, he appeared nude at the top of the stairs and bellowed, "What can I do about these?!" as he bent over and spread his cheeks to show the shocked group his pesky hemorrhoids.

Michael helped me become fluent in the gruff Italian spoken by his parents, working-class immigrants from Sicily. Aside from him, I wouldn't befriend anybody who spoke English, so that I could better learn the local lingo. My Italian teacher was a skinny old lady with dyed black hair who taught lots of wonderful outdated expressions, such as "It's raining like God sent it" and "I'm so mad I'm gonna put my hands in my hair." It was fun to use such old-fashioned jargon alongside the modern Roman slang I'd learned, like the playful jibe *Mortaci tua*, which loosely translates to "I hope your friends and family who are dead are rotting in hell." I also picked up a lot by watching the news, though I often flipped over to the omnipresent cheesy variety shows to watch surreal musical numbers, such as one with buxom babes doing an interpretive dance to "Volare" on the wing of an airplane as it made its way down the runway. Communicating was incredibly frustrating for the first few months, but one day I awoke and found I could suddenly hold my own with the natives. The trick was not to try to follow each word—thereby getting totally lost—but to listen to everything someone had to say and then patch together the words you recognized to figure out what the point was. The lasting benefit was that I became a slightly more patient listener on the whole.

After class, Michael and I would roam the streets to get to know our fair city, with its imposing architecture and lively inhabitants, gorging on cheap potato pizza, roasted chestnuts, and fresh coconut wedges sold by sidewalk vendors. Italy is the easiest place to be vegetarian; you never need to scrutinize menus, as virtually every restaurant serves numerous pizza and pasta dishes without meat. One night, as we strolled by the Pantheon, we happened upon an animal rights exhibit complete with a graphic slide show visible throughout the square, organized by the Lega Anti-Vivisezione. I offered to volunteer, and they invited me to their headquarters; my first assignment was to translate a report on the laboratory raid at the City of Hope—the one my friend Connie had helped scope out—from an American newsletter called *PETA News*. Small world. I also helped plaster CANCELED stickers over circus posters near the Colosseum, where the sadistic ritual of tormenting exotic animals for public merriment got its start.

Since most Italians live at home with their very large families until they marry, they can't easily invite you over to hang out, so our apartment became a getaway and party pad for anyone bearing food or booze. This was a blessing, as Michael and I, the destitute duo of our program, had to get by on $50 a week. Among our regular guests were two vibrant, penniless punk rockers named Gina and Eleonora, whom we met in a bar in Trastevere. They helped us understand Rome's raunchy dialect, brought us on hitchhiking adventures to the lakes and hills outside the city, and introduced us to Rome's thriving underground clubs. No matter how late we stayed out, I was always up early, ready to explore more ruins, while groggy Michael would roll over in his matching twin bed and plead, "Take pictures with my camera so I can pretend I was there, too."

The most memorable underground "scene" was the cold, musty catacombs, where dead bodies from centuries past are displayed in various states of decay, clad in the spiffiest clothes of their time. At first these tombs were exclusively for monks, but they soon became popular among well-to-do Italians who didn't want to be buried or cremated, never to be seen again. For the right price, they could have themselves chemically preserved and displayed on the walls of subterranean crypts. In some cases, all that remain are hardened veins, bones, and bonnets. Although these gothic enclaves aren't prime tourist attractions, you can buy macabre postcards of the finely dressed stiffs; I stocked up and send them out as birthday cards to select friends even today, with the short greeting, "One year closer to the grave."

One evening, Michael burst through the door clutching a box from an expensive bakery. He breathlessly called me into the kitchen, where he popped open a bottle of Spumante and proudly proclaimed he'd found a way to make some money: prostitution. He'd been walking in the sprawling Villa Borghese park, where he often chitchatted around a boom box with his gay friends, when a man pulled over and propositioned him with a fifty-thousand-lire bill, which was then about fifty dollars. Michael was both flabbergasted and flattered and quickly hopped in to consummate the deal, awkwardly maneuvering around the steering wheel.

As adventurous as I liked to think I was, I was shocked by his antics—but at the same time intrigued. It made me reflect on my own sexuality, or rather the total lack of it. I had just started to sense that I was no longer the repulsive pariah I had been in high school. For one thing, since becoming a vegetarian, I had dropped forty pounds. Second, unlike in conservative Orange County, the punk look was considered the height of fashion in Rome in the early 1980s; instead of jeering and punching us, people on the street smiled and waved. The reactions couldn't have been more different, or baffling. One day on the bus, some girls who assumed I didn't speak Italian dared each other to say hello to the "cute foreigner." I sheepishly glanced around to see who they might be talking about and found that I was the only other passenger. I forced a smile but felt incredibly awkward; I had grown so comfortable being the object of scorn that I had no idea how to handle lust. I continually shut the topic out of my mind, figuring I was too self-conscious to make any first moves anyway, and hoping someone pushy would come along to break the ice.

Italians being the frisky bunch they are, I was soon presented with such an opportunity—but it wasn't at all the way I would have predicted. One evening, as I walked along ritzy Via Veneto with spiky white hair and wearing an olive-colored military trench coat, a man in a Fiat slowed down and asked if I wanted a ride. The expression on his face suggested that he wasn't simply a Good Samaritan. As I looked around, considering his offer and what it might entail, he reached over and opened the passenger door. I nonchalantly got in. At first, excited to have a car at my disposal, I wanted to suggest we go sightseeing or stop for a drink on Appia Antica, but I grew nervous and could only think of Michael's recent sordid experience. As we sped off, the nice man put his hand on my knee.

The cliché, "When in Rome," popped into my head, so I masked my anxiety with a dead serious demeanor, turned to the driver, and said, *"Si paga prima"* (you pay first). He nodded matter-of-factly and asked, *"Cuanto?"*

"Fifty thousand lire," I replied assertively, pretending like I was rough trade rather than a green teen. He nodded in agreement and pulled out the cash. The awkwardness I'd always felt in any sexual situation was quickly replaced by a strange adrenaline rush. I tried to keep my cool demeanor, but inside I was ecstatic to finally be facing my clumsy disdain for sex. My heart pounded as we parked in the Villa Borghese and started to mess around. I felt like I was suddenly in some trashy made-for-TV movie. When it became evident that I wasn't prepared for our interaction to amount to much, mostly due to my fear of AIDS, my client offered to double my money, but I refused. We finished our business, and afterward he dropped me off near the top of the Spanish Steps.

I decided to walk home instead of taking the bus, as my mind was buzzing; part of me felt like I should be ashamed, but at the same time I was elated to have finally "done it," even if it was in a car, with a stranger, for money. Lame excuses kept popping into my head, like "I'm here to study history, and this is the world's oldest profession." With a wild smirk on my face, I strode down Corso Vittorio and stopped at the same bakery where Michael had splurged after turning his first trick. Now it was my turn to bring home pastries and a bottle of Spumante.

Michael and most of the other students from the States went home after the fall semester to carry on with their studies at American University in Washington, D.C., but I was determined to stay in Italy as long as possible, especially now that I had figured out how to make ends meet. But I could no longer afford the place Michael and I had shared, so I checked the classifieds and found an apartment in dusty old Piazza Vittorio with three guys from southern Italy. My share of the rent was $90 a month (or two quick trips to the Villa Borghese).

I wanted to get a proper part-time job, but couldn't without European citizenship. About the only approved profession for overseas foreigners was "actor" or "model"—many of whom I had befriended at clubs and parties. Some of them said I should try breaking into the business, but I laughed off the suggestion. As the months wore on, however, and my self-confidence improved, largely due to the odd gig as a gigolo, I became more open to the idea. Anna Kanakis, a girl I met who'd recently been Miss Italy and also appeared in movies and ads, invited me to her sleek apartment to discuss the matter. She told me I needed a portfolio and gave me the phone number of a photographer friend with a studio near the Vatican who said he'd shoot me as a favor. Anna showed me pictures he'd taken of her writhing on the ground in full-length furs.

"As long as I don't have to wear the furs," I told her.

She laughed. "Oh, sorry, I forgot." Anna also arranged a meeting for me with her agency, Caremoli, which had offices in both Milan and Rome. With my hair toned down to a normal blond shade and a set of barely adequate black-and-white pictures under my arm, I anxiously rode the subway to meet them.

"Ah, Anna's friend," said the insincere man who came to greet me at Caremoli's reception desk. "We'd be happy to represent you—just leave your pictures and make sure my secretary knows how to get in touch." He shook my hand and nodded me out. Two weeks passed, and they never called. I thought it would seem ungrateful to whine to Anna, so I complained about "my agent" to some models at a party.

"This is typical," said Haye, a tall, bony guy from Holland, whose promiscuous girlfriend had just landed a big bridal campaign. "They didn't even tell you about the big Fiat tryout tomorrow?"

"What Fiat tryout?" I pried. He told me the name of the studio, and I immediately decided to crash the audition.

The lobby was clogged with dozens and dozens of suave European models aiming to land the new television campaign for the Fiat Panda—and I felt as out-of-place as an albino at the beach. At the check-in desk, you had to sign your name and list your agency. "Caremoli," I wrote. The long line of hopefuls snaked into a studio in which producers ordered each person, one by one, to stand against a brightly lit wall, as if to be executed. A voice from a dark control room asked, "What's your name," "How are you," "Please smile," "Turn to the right, now to the left," then "Thank you." It was an unnervingly brief screen test, and most of the models struck the poses but looked awkward as they mechanically followed instructions. As I inched closer to my turn before the firing squad, I struggled to figure out how I could set myself apart. Instead of just saying my name and "I'm fine," I hastily tried to think of a lively anecdote I could relay, in the course of which I would smile and turn every which way unprompted, and then thank them at the end.

"What's your name?" quizzed the faceless voice in Italian.

"Dan Mathews."

"How are you?"

"Fine now," I replied, "but last night I bummed a ride home from a party with a bunch of junkies who shot up right in front of me under the bridge near the tomb of Augustus. I don't mind needles at the doctor's office, but to see these guys jab themselves in a dark car was too much. I also worried that the cops might see us, so I jumped out and walked home along the Tiber, as it was such a beautiful night. Thanks for asking. How are you?"

"*Bene, grazie,*" said the mysterious voice. "Next!" As I walked out, I glanced toward the guys waiting behind me to gauge any reaction, but they quickly averted their eyes, not wanting to add to my humiliation. I maintained a smile, but felt like an utter imbecile.

Over the next week I tried to put the embarrassing episode—and my modeling and acting aspirations—out of my head and focus on my studies, but I couldn't help but feel depressed. I only had a few hundred dollars (and no credit cards) to last me six months. The novelty of working the streets had worn off, and I feared that I'd soon be forced to return to Ronald Reagan's America, my overseas adventure reaching a premature ending. Late one gray February afternoon, I glumly walked home the long way, trudging through the crumbling Roman Forum and down some side streets. I pushed open the heavy wooden doors to my grubby building, dragged my feet up the stairs to the fourth floor, keyed into my apartment, and hollered *ciao* to whoever might be home. My roommate Maurizio yelled back that I had a message near the phone.

"Call Caremoli urgently," it read. "Fiat needs you at Cinecittá this Friday."

I started trembling so much that I could barely dial the number. My suddenly enthusiastic agent informed me that I got the big job and that it would pay two million lire, which would cover my rent through spring and summer with about $1,500 left over. He also asked me to rush to the office to get a schedule of other auditions they wanted to send me on. My mood boomeranged so much I became dizzy, a feeling that was compounded by the lie that I told my agent:

"Of course I can drive a stick shift."

In the silly spot, I'm behind the wheel of a little white Fiat in a flurry of fake snow on a set of the Manhattan skyline while a Muzak version of Frank Sinatra's "New York, New York" blares. As I drive slowly past the camera, I lean out and say the Italian equivalent of "The snow plow might be frozen over, but my Panda always runs!" I then flash the international symbol for "Okay" while unwittingly hitting a fire hydrant, which was rigged to spray water all over the set. Never having driven a stick shift before, I nearly destroyed the set and ran over a technician. After a few dangerous takes, the director told me to take the car out of gear and let a stagehand push me from behind, kneeling in order to remain off camera.

"Fine," I said. "How do you take it out of gear?" We finally finished, and I breathed a big sigh of relief. Before leaving Cinecittà, I wandered around, wondering which sound stage Fellini had used for *Satyricon* and stopped by the studio bar for a euphoric celebratory drink.

My good luck continued the next week, when the film we shot was somehow ruined in processing; as my agent was now active, I had gone to Milan to audition for a chocolate commercial, but Fiat flew me back to Rome for a reshoot— and to fork over a million more lire. In a matter of weeks I had gone from hitchhiker living on dollar slices of pizza to high flyer sipping drinks in Alitalia's first class cabin. The commercial, which was shown not only on TV but in movie theaters, led to more work, including a fashion show on a runway erected on the Circus Maximus and a music video for a British group called Matt Bianco. The singer was a Polish girl named Basia who would find worldwide success years later as a solo artist. In the video, I wear a black beret and sit in an overstuffed chair with my friend Monica, a Roman midget with a black bob wearing a kimono; all we do is laugh and click glasses before the camera pans to other Roman scenesters hired for the party sequence.

Before heading to the music video shoot, since we were all gussied up, a bunch of us sped around to various picturesque Roman squares to shoot black-and-white movies of ourselves with a rickety old Super 8 camera I often lugged around. As I filmed my trendy friends gawking and waving at Piazza del Popolo, I noticed a familiar-looking older gentleman sitting near us by one of the columns. It was Federico Fellini, my favorite director, alone, just people-watching. Like obnoxious Mr. Paparazzo from *La Dolce Vita*, I kept the film running, pointed the camera at him, and shouted, "Fellini! Fellini!" Then we engulfed him and hollered out which of his films we liked best (*Amarcord* for me). He smiled warmly and said he loved our vintage outfits.

That spring, a comedy director from Naples named Ciro Ipolito cast me as a gay Indian with shimmering blue war paint in his Western satire *Arrapaho*. Even though I only had a small supporting role, they sent a car to my hovel each morning to drive me to the set in a forest two hours outside of Rome. In the movie, I marry a male squaw from a neighboring tribe—perhaps the first on-screen gay wedding. In other scenes, I leap from a tepee, struggle to wade upstream in a river, and take part in a tribal ritual around a totem pole shaped like a giant dick; the film didn't win any awards at Cannes but was hugely popular in Italy, where it still runs on television.

When I was out on the town and people asked what I did, I never said "student," as I was petrified to be lumped in with the rumpled, earnest backpack brigade. I felt equally

uneasy saying "actor" or "model"; the correct answer would
have been "fool for hire," but I replied "vegetarian" because
I was more excited to talk about animal rights than babble
about fashion or Fiats. I was increasingly riveted by the material I had started gathering for my senior thesis on animals in
the ancient world, particularly how they were regarded by
philosophers. There's probably nothing drearier to bring up
at a party. Some polite person would comment, "Wow, what
did ancient philosophers have to say about animals?" I'd
invariably respond by quoting Plutarch's first-century essay,
"On Eating Flesh," in the same way others might recite a
monologue from a movie they've seen a million times:

> *I marvel at what sort of feeling, mind, or reason the*
> *man had who first polluted his mouth with gore and*
> *allowed his lips to touch the flesh of a murdered*
> *being; who spread his table with the mangled forms of*
> *dead bodies and claimed as his food beings endowed*
> *with movement, perception and voice. How could his*
> *eyes endure the spectacle of the flayed and dismem-*
> *bered limbs? How could his sense of smell endure the*
> *horrid stench? How, I ask, was his taste not sickened*
> *by contact with festering wounds, blood and juices?*

"Hors d'oeuvres, anyone?"

Five hundred years before Plutarch, there was Pythagoras, a prominent Greek philosopher so disturbed by animal
cruelty that he paid fishermen to throw their catch back in
the sea. "Alas, how immoral to swallow flesh into our own
flesh, to fatten our greedy bodies by cramming in other bodies," he wrote.

Whenever anybody suggested that animals don't have

souls, I'd point out that the Latin (and Italian) word for soul is *anima,* which simply means "self-propelled form of life." Add an *l,* and what have you got? "Animals share with us the privilege of having a soul," wrote Pythagoras, who said that eating meat or participating in any other kind of animal abuse harms your soul and your health. Three thousand years before a flood of medical studies connected meat to heart disease, cancer, and obesity, he wrote, "Humans dig their graves with their teeth." I wondered why these old, sensible observations hadn't instantly caught on like other ancient ideas, such as the wheel or pizza, but were instead relegated to the "ahead of their time" pile, like homosexuality and democracy.

Eventually, I came to think that if I found myself instinctively proclaiming I was an animal activist, maybe I should be more than an occasional volunteer. With my shady agent lining up more and more auditions and urging me to put school on hold, I reflected on why I had come to Italy. It wasn't to break into show business. Thrilling as it was to suddenly have money, eat in restaurants, and go on weekend trips, I began to look at acting and modeling much as I did my stints as a dancing Christmas tree and a street hustler: a brief, chance diversion from a far more fulfilling career as some kind of do-gooder.

So, as much as I loved Rome, I took a deep breath, dyed my hair Hawaiian Punch red, and made a surprise visit to Caremoli to collect the last installment of lire from the spaghetti Western in order to move to Washington, D.C. I decided to remain in school and transfer my credits from Rome to American University, where I'd have my history degree at age twenty. Then I'd be free to do anything.

Roller skating with Ingrid in Maryland.

CHAPTER 5

A Reluctant Revolutionary

In the summer of 1985, Reagan implored Gorbachev to tear down the Berlin Wall, Rock Hudson died of AIDS, Route 66 was decertified, and I took a job as receptionist with a young organization called People for the Ethical Treatment of Animals. The group was so unknown to the general public that I dealt with calls from a doggie stage mother who thought we were People for *Theatrical* Treatment of Animals and from a man whose accent I couldn't place who thought we were People for the *Ethnic* Treatment of Animals.

I almost quit within a week because the sandal-clad young woman I commuted with chomped on organic carrots for much of the thirty-minute drive. Each muggy morning, as I waited fearfully near my D.C. apartment for her to pick me up en route to PETA's house-cum-headquarters in Bethesda, Maryland, I'd pray she'd switched to bananas, Pop Tarts, even beef jerky—anything that didn't crunch so loudly so early in the morning.

Carpool friction aside, I was anxious to tackle what I hoped would be a career as a full-time animal activist, putting all other odd jobs behind me. I wanted to get up every day and help change the world. When the job at PETA materialized as I was about to graduate, I was ecstatic. I'd be earning a living by living my dream. Upon being told that the starting salary for this dream was $10,400, I was flabbergasted; it was like winning on the *$10,000 Pyramid,* plus $400.

Since the rent in my timeworn, one-room, non-air-conditioned, kitchen-free abode was only $216, I was now rich enough to fix it up. The splintery hardwood floor got covered with roll after roll after roll of cheap marble contact paper, which, friends said, gave my entire hovel the feel of a clean cabinet. I kept it looking good by requiring visitors to remove their shoes. In thrift shops, I found a wobbly atomic-era coffee table and a bright orange steel tool shelf to hold my record player, tiny TV, and books. I sat and slept on a black foam sofa, above which hung a giant, fluorescent finger painting I'd found in an alley. My "stove" consisted of a small hot pot, which I'd use to heat a can of spinach and then rinse in the bathroom sink to make instant coffee.

PETA founder Ingrid Newkirk didn't hire me for my decorating or culinary skills, but for my upbeat attitude and the accomplishments of the animal rights club I'd started at American University with my friend Melissa, such as halting the poisoning of AU's pigeons with Avitrol, a chemical that shatters the birds' nervous systems and causes them to flutter and squirm as if caught in a lawn mower before they drop dead. Clippings from the *AU Eagle* had made their way to PETA.

"Well done with the pigeons," Ingrid said, firmly shaking my hand as I sat at her desk in the small converted bedroom.

Ingrid's back was to the window, the morning light radiating around her and onto me, making me feel as if I were onstage or under interrogation. I was nervous, wanting to explain how dedicated I was without seeming overeager. I also felt a bit out of place with my short, spiky white hair and red checkerboard shirt; most of the nine-person staff then was low-key and longhaired.

"Either you didn't know about us, or we didn't know about you," Ingrid said, smiling as she leafed through the articles. It wasn't official yet, but from that point on, I knew I had a job.

I was relieved to find that Ingrid—a bottle-blond Brit then in her early thirties—was whimsical and irreverent in person, much breezier than the "tough cookie" I'd seen in television debates. We discovered a mutual fascination with *Pee Wee's Playhouse* and lawn ornaments and connected personally as well as professionally. In the 1970s, Ingrid had been married to a race-car driver and had a career in the stock market until, one day, while looking to adopt a dog, she happened into the squalid dog pound near the U.S. Capitol. First, she volunteered to help clean the place up. Then, abandoning her comfortable life, she became D.C.'s first female "pound master"—but refused to allow them to change the title to "pound mistress," as she thought it made her sound like a diet guru. Soon Ingrid was named director of the Washington Humane Society, tidying it beyond recognition and stopping the shelter's sale of refugee animals to laboratories before going on to found PETA in 1980. *Washingtonian* magazine named Ingrid "Washingtonian of the Year" in 1981.

"Since you are familiar with so many animal issues,"

Ingrid said, "we could really use you as our 'public liaison'—to answer people's questions when they call or write in." I soon realized that this meant "receptionist."

Sitting at my desk in the basement, I answered telephone queries from activists, students, and the public, including an earnest Southern woman desperate to find a celebrated baby monkey rescued from a laboratory, where his eyes had been sewn shut. She insisted on squiring him to a religious revival to have him healed. The letter writers tended to be more composed, inquiring about everything from motel chains that allowed dogs to which brands of toothpaste weren't tested by being squirted into rabbits' eyes. As these were precomputer days, I hunted and pecked responses to dozens of letters each day on a clunky old typewriter with a lazy *u*. It might not sound revolutionary, but I loved it.

Sometimes, I'd hear a commotion coming down the stairs and look outside to see Ingrid trundling Ms. Bea, a walruslike mutt whose rear end was paralyzed; Ingrid acted as Bea's back legs, hunching over and propelling her like a wheelbarrow. I'd watch in wonder as Ingrid squeezed her furry friend's behind to make a dog-doo sundae on the lawn, exclaiming, "Good girl!" to an appreciative Bea as she cleaned her up.

Aside from Ingrid, I didn't have much in common with many of my early, earthy colleagues, nice as they were. We shared substance but not style, which seems a silly concern now but was a dilemma for a trendy twenty-year-old. I wasn't interested in this week's bargain at the food co-op, hadn't read the latest *Mother Jones*, and didn't hang out exclusively with vegans.

·   ·   ·

During my second week, Ingrid blindsided me with the question, "Have you ever been arrested?" I hesitated. Was this a truth test?

"Yes," I finally admitted. "Once. For shoplifting Queen singles. In junior high."

"What I mean," she said, rolling her eyes, "is *would* you get arrested—for animals?"

"What for, exactly?"

"The charge would probably be trespassing. Just a misdemeanor, and that's all I can tell you." I had never considered getting arrested on purpose. I was intrigued, yet cautious of getting too involved too quickly, so I wouldn't commit without knowing more.

A secret action was being planned; anxious activists from all over were calling for directions to PETA from the interstate and the airport, and my higher-ups were conducting suspicious closed-door discussions. Naturally, I tried to eavesdrop but still couldn't figure out what was going on. At the end of the week, I was frustrated and clueless when Ingrid asked me to be at work an hour early the following Monday morning.

I walked through the door at 8 a.m. to an empty house, except for a strange woman on the phone in Ingrid's room. I walked upstairs as she finished her call.

"Hi, I'm Vicki from Toronto Humane," said the smiling redhead as she rose from her chair. "I came down to help with press for the occupation. You must be Dan."

"Occupation?" I asked. She looked at me with surprise. "I guess I'm too new to trust."

"Well, now you can know," she said. "This morning, a hundred PETA members are occupying the grants office at the National Institutes of Health just up the road until NIH stops funding the Gennarelli head-injury lab in Pennsylvania. You know the place."

I knew it well. It was the cover story on the most recent PETA quarterly and had even made *60 Minutes*. Much of my college dormitory had watched it in shock in the TV lounge a few months earlier. Thomas Gennarelli, a top researcher at the University of Pennsylvania, led federally funded experi-ments—which were filmed—in which giggling, smoking Ivy League medical students gave baboons hallucinogenic drugs, strapped the animals to a table, then cemented their heads into helmets attached to a hydraulic device. At the flip of a switch, the machine blasted the primates' heads so violently that their bound bodies flailed like rag dolls, causing brain damage intended to mimic car crash or football injuries, after which the experimenters pounded the animals' heads out of the helmets with a hammer and screwdriver. Joking around as if in a home movie, the researchers ridiculed the dazed baboons, dangling one aloft by his dislocated shoulder and quipping into the camera, "You better hope the antivivisec-tion people don't get a hold of this film."

Word had gotten out about the videos, and on Memorial Day of 1984 the underground Animal Liberation Front broke into the lab, stole the tapes, and sent them to PETA. PETA catapulted the case into the national news by coordinating a campaign urging the Reagan administration to halt the lab's million-dollar annual grant. Thousands of protest letters poured in—many from senators, members of Congress, and doctors—yet NIH, the lumbering branch of our government charged with overseeing medical research, wouldn't budge—except to defend the school, the researcher, and itself.

Almost every social or political movement has a watershed moment in which it transcends the fringe and begins to enter the mainstream. It's never the issues themselves but how the powers that be react to them that tips the scales, causing the masses to take notice and sympathize with the oppressed. For the civil rights movement it was when Alabama police throttled peaceful protestors on national television, and for gays it was when officers launched one too many unprovoked raids at the Stonewall bar, causing a weekend of Greenwich Village riots. Though not as ballyhooed, for animals it was when footage of Gennarelli's sadistic baboon experiments aired coast-to-coast, and instead of condemning the obvious atrocity, NIH said it was more concerned with finding and jailing those who broke into the laboratory to steal the tapes and make them public. Columnists were outraged at the "cruel cronyism," Paul Harvey blasted NIH in his national radio program, and a wave of everyday people who had never before thought of themselves as animal advocates called to join this maverick new group, PETA. It was one of the reasons I finally decided to seek work there, and now here I was, practically at the center of the action.

"We need you to hand out news releases to reporters outside Building 31 at NIH, with the updated list of protesters and their hometowns," Vicki instructed me in Ingrid's office. I was happy to finally be in on the Big Secret but instantly regretted that I hadn't agreed to join the troops only a mile away.

NIH is a sprawling maze of hospitals, laboratories, offices, and a spaceshiplike medical library, all impeccably landscaped. I sprinted through the quiet complex, wondering which buildings held animals. As I turned a corner, I could see TV vans clogging the hilly, circular driveway, which led to Building 31, a long fourteen-story structure with big windows. Being inexperienced, I felt as if I was breaking the law just passing out news releases, and my heart raced excitedly.

I hurried up the driveway and spotted Ingrid and handsome PETA cofounder Alex Pacheco giving interviews in the lobby. A few protesters stood behind them with poster-size photos of the terrified baboons from the controversial video. Others were streaming into elevators bound for the eighth floor, where the actual target office was. Surprisingly, there were only a few security guards, and they seemed more preoccupied with the news cameras than with the protesters.

Ingrid waved me over. "You have the releases?" I nodded and asked if I could help with anything else. "Yes—want to join us upstairs?" I distributed the releases to the dozen or so reporters and TV crews, and then jumped into an elevator with my new bosses. Chanting echoed from above. When the bell rang on eight, the doors parted and the chanting transformed into cheers for Ingrid and Alex.

Itchy with excitement, I moved on to see the sights and the hundred or so protesters scattered throughout several freshly evacuated office suites. I ran into Alex Pacheco's mother, Ann, a sweet and goofy lady from Ohio, whose beige blouse was so wet that I thought the police had fired a water cannon at her. She explained that en route to the raid she had spilled coffee all over herself and tried to rinse the stain out in the bathroom. I met several people I'd spoken to on the phone, including a stripper from Philadelphia, a veterinarian from San Francisco, a lobbyist from Iowa, a high school student from Maine, a philosophy professor from North Carolina, and a Jewish mother from down the block. Completing my rounds, I found Ingrid in the swank executive office doing my job—answering phones.

"Good morning, and thank you for calling NIH," she said in her dainty British accent. "This office will remain closed until NIH stops funding the hideous baboon experiments at the University of Pennsylvania. Have a pleasant day." Click.

Finished with my tour, I joined in the ongoing chants near the elevator bank, which soon had me cringing. "We speak for the animals, their pain and ours are one; we'll fight for the animals, until their rights are won." I'll never shake those plodding, whiny words from my memory. Chants are crucial in keeping people's spirits up at protests, but no matter the movement, they so often sound like an overearnest dirge. They're most effective when they're funny. At an AIDS march at the Supreme Court, when paranoid police donned rubber gloves before arresting people, we chanted, "They'll see you on the news—your gloves don't match your shoes!"

Crowds gathered below to gawk at the signs and posters hanging from the windows and to listen to graphic explanations of why we were there via bullhorns. Sirens wailed onto the scene, but strangely, no cops burst onto the eighth floor.

"When the police arrive, don't fight with them," Ingrid and Alex instructed. "Go limp, chant, or go quietly, but don't antagonize them. That's not why we're here." Among the troops, a prim housewife in peachy lip gloss nodded in approval, but an unshaven biker didn't seem convinced.

As the day wore on, some protesters planted themselves around desks and sofas and got to know each other, while others—me included—grew restless. Our lawyer, Gary Francione, a University of Pennsylvania law professor, explained that NIH might wait until we all got tired and left to avoid arresting us, thus keeping the story small and local and the public pressure off. That meant Ingrid and Alex's job was to keep everybody there, which proved difficult, as everyone had expected to be booked and released in time for dinner. The peace-loving chants began competing with bitter phone arguments as spouses called to explain why they might not be home tonight—or tomorrow night. Yuppies phoned their offices to call in sick for Tuesday. Others gave up and slunk down the stairwell. I thought of slipping away, too, not because I had a ball and chain or unruly boss to fret over, but because I'd made plans to "judge" the Miss Universe pageant with a couch full of friends.

We made our own soiree that night in Building 31, which was like a stilted slumber party until two guys broke into the executive office liquor cabinet. I excitedly dashed for a glass, but stopped short when Ingrid yelled at them to put everything back. Trudging around in sad sobriety, I surveyed the muttering, mixed bunch. I was reminded of the scene in *Close Encounters of the Third Kind* in which the motley group of total strangers who shared a vision and desperately raced to the UFO-bound mountain suddenly found themselves quietly locked up and wondering what the hell they were all doing there together.

We worried that the police might take us away in the middle of the night, since the cameras were long gone, so people were appointed to take turns monitoring the elevator bank and stairwell. I shared the night shift with an intense, strapping, bearded Vietnam vet who made extra cash posing nude for art classes and a demure, bespectacled nurse from Delaware, who was worried about leaving her ailing father alone. I listened and nodded in sincere sympathy, too embarrassed to disclose that my biggest worry was missing the Dolly Parton special on HBO later that week.

We expected canisters of tear gas but instead got gusts of Freon; NIH's master plan consisted of trying to freeze us out by cranking up the air-conditioning. We opened windows to let in the balmy summer air, but the office remained icy. Since I wasn't accustomed to air conditioning at home, the place felt like a meat locker to me. Before each of us claimed a patch of polyester carpet to sleep on, we took down curtains to use as blankets. One guy wrapped himself in the American flag, causing a minor squabble with the Vietnam vet. I found shelter under a desk and pulled a phone down to call friends and my parents to whisper a spirited report on the siege, just in case they saw it on the news and got worried.

"Hi, Dad? You know the job I just started at that animal group? Well, we've all just barricaded ourselves in a government office." He and my stepmother spoke cautiously, as if I'd joined a cult, warning me to be careful. My mom, on the other hand, wasn't sure we were going far enough and suggested we strap NIH workers to desktops and threaten to bash them like the baboons unless they stopped the experiments. Well after midnight, as the crickets gossiped in the bushes below, I went fetal to keep warm under the desk and fell asleep.

I was jolted awake at dawn to the sound of a crackling bullhorn, thwacking my noggin on the desk and suddenly feeling like a freshly abducted Patty Hearst. An irritating early riser had decided to initiate a debate with a janitor arriving for work eight stories down. Thankfully, somebody confiscated her bullhorn, but by now we were all up. Ingrid, looking like a scarecrow with her slept-on hair, gave a strained pep talk and explained we might be here all week. "We cannot give up," she pleaded to the assembly of zombies.

We had barely wiped the sleep from our eyes when NIH security guards arrived, accompanied by the police. Unfortunately, they hadn't come to arrest us, just to inspect the overrun offices and make sure we hadn't ransacked the place. To inflate our ever-dwindling numbers, we declared certain rooms off limits, lying to the authorities that old ladies were still asleep or that young girls were changing. Our lawyer arranged for fruit, hummus sandwiches, and shampoo to be brought in. Following a quick snack and a pseudo-scrub, we pretended to be rejuvenated enough to belt out slogans as workers began to arrive below.

After about ten minutes of nauseating chants, my sleep-deprived vigor had drained away, and when nobody was looking, I made a snap decision to scram into the stairwell. Hurdling down three steps at a time, I thought, *Enough!* I was just beginning to accept the fact that I'd be with my PETA comrades nine to five—how could I so suddenly be expected to endure them twenty-four/seven? I flung open the emergency exit on the far side of the building and turned my face skyward to marvel at the sunshine and feel the July humidity hug all the Freon out of me. Catching my breath, I reasoned that since the occupation might go on all week, I'd simply unwind a bit at home and slip back in later that day.

On the subway home, the exhilaration I felt at being free from the aggravations of the protest started mixing with guilt for having ditched my colleagues and, worse, of course, the baboons. I put it out of my mind and instead thought of the long bath and calming Bobbie Gentry records that awaited me. I trudged into my stale apartment building, bid

a weary hi to the yellow-finger-nailed Ethiopian superin-
tendent in the rickety elevator, and pondered the surprise
twenty-four-hour odyssey I'd just been on. How it made me
relish the comforts of even my ramshackle hole of a home. I
tossed my keys on the coffee table and glanced down as they
clinked atop the PETA magazine. A pulverized baboon with
wires coming out of his head glanced back. I quickly looked
away and pressed Play on my answering machine: a dinner
date was confirmed, a friend asked why I wasn't at dollar
vodka night, and someone wondered if I was involved in the
NIH sit-in she'd seen on the news and wished us well. I
started to reach for the phone but froze. What would I say?
*Yeah, I was there, it was great, but I bailed because I didn't
want to miss a TV show?*

Feeling pathetic, I cranked on the bath. Any bravado I
had felt about finally being a full-time firebrand was crushed
by shame at having deserted the battle at NIH. After years of
yearning to be on the front lines, I'd allowed trivial annoy-
ances to pry me away from one of the most exciting experiences of my life and let down the people I truly admired.
Sitting down to remove my shoes, I looked again at the magazine with the battered baboon on the cover and uneasily
forced myself to reconsider my priorities. It took me about
four seconds. I tore off my clothes, took a short shower, and
left as quickly as I had arrived, changing into a green hospital scrub left by a doctor I'd had a fling with in order to pen-
etrate security back at NIH.

I had no problem getting back up to the eighth floor.
Ingrid hid her disappointment that I'd left by simply thank-
ing me for coming back. Many of the twenty or so remaining
protesters thought that I'd been napping in another room. I

hoped they thought that again over the next few days when, thanks to my surgical shirt, I was able to momentarily disappear to have coffee in the NIH cafeteria and read the *Washington Post*. If I were ever kidnapped, my captors would surely shoot me rather than tolerate Mr. Fidget.

The scene I returned to was much different than the one I had arrived at Monday morning. The hundred exuberant protesters jamming several offices had eroded into a bored and weary skeleton crew, which stayed more out of respect for Ingrid and Alex than for any true hope that we could stop the baboon experiments. That was a good enough reason for me, too, and not just because I wanted to nullify the poor impression I must have made on my new employers.

By Tuesday evening, the phones were cut off, and, this being before cell phones, our only connection to the outside world was through Alex Pacheco's walkie-talkie and a tiny old portable television. When NIH declared that no more food could be brought in, our crafty attorney smuggled in a fifty-foot rope, which we dangled out a window for volunteers to tie to a food basket before we hoisted it back up. The rope trick kept the story alive, and watching each other in fuzzy black-and-white on the news at eleven cheered us up. Although the occupation was well covered in Washington, the story was dwarfed nationally by President Reagan's sudden surgery to remove polyps from his colon, a procedure happening directly across from NIH at the Naval Hospital. More than once, we fluttered our arms out the window, hollering, "Over here!" to aloof reporters in a CNN van. How frustrating that some stations wouldn't air the baboon-bashing video because it was "too graphic" yet had no problem flooding the airwaves with X-rays of our commander in chief's diseased digestive tract.

Finally, early Wednesday morning, three days after the occupation began, we received a crucial boost when the *Today* show made good on an offer for Ingrid to appear and plead our case. She sneaked out for the coast-to-coast chat with Jane Pauley via satellite from NBC's nearby studio, and the producers were gutsy enough to show the baboon video during the breakfast hour. Watching the segment on the contraband portable television as if it were the lunar landing, we prayed that someone in a position to help was tuning in.

As if sent from heaven, or maybe to play a cruel joke, a man in a suit came up our sequestered stairwell later that same day, saying he worked for Margaret Heckler, Reagan's secretary of health and human services—NIH's boss. He explained that Heckler had seen our protest on the news, but that NIH refused to hand over the infamous baboon tape. Ingrid and Alex gave him the video, along with a folder bulging with damning critiques of the experiment from various medical experts. We crossed our fatigued fingers and hoped that he was authentic.

Just about a dozen of us remained Thursday morning when writer/protestor Jim Mason and his girlfriend Nora decided to leave and begin their long drive back to Connecticut. He planned to pen a lively account of PETA's valiant, if unsuccessful, efforts to save the baboons. As they wearily drove north on Interstate 95 with the radio on to keep them alert, Jim and Nora were wrenched from their bucket seats by a national CBS News report that the Reagan administration would surrender to animal activists and end the University of Pennsylvania head-injury experiments. Just after Jim had left, Margaret Heckler's man had returned to fetch Alex for an urgent meeting with humiliated NIH officials. Heckler, sickened by the video, had scheduled a noon-time news conference to announce she would intervene and shut down the lab.

Things seemed to shift into a dreamlike slow motion when the incredible news was confirmed. Ingrid announced we'd give back the eighth floor tidier than we'd found it, then rushed downstairs to call PETA so that the media could be alerted that we'd be streaming out of Building 31 in an hour. Amid outbursts of emotion, heightened by our lack of sleep, we cleaned and dusted the office and rehung drapes and flags. From the windows we could see news crews, PETA volunteers, and curious NIH workers gathering outside.

Shortly after noon, the chants began one last time in the elevator bank, but this time, instead of cringing, I cried. We filed out slowly, one by one, as if it were still important that our numbers seem inflated, holding aloft the heartbreaking posters of the baboons. At last they had won their reprieve. Alex made a brief speech praising Margaret Heckler and blasting NIH. Then began the media frenzy. One reporter asked me what the occupation signified.

"It shows there's a way of beating the bureaucrats," I responded. The quote, along with a headline declaring PRO-TESTERS' SIT-IN HALTS RESEARCH, appeared in *USA Today*, which impressed my dad. The win was so significant that we made all three national network news shows that evening. "Medical research is important," said Reagan cabinet member Heckler. "But so are the animal victims of this research." She was soon reassigned overseas as the ambassador to Ireland.

I began the week as a receptionist and finished it feeling like a real revolutionary. Inspired by being near the core of such a strategic triumph and empowered by the fact that my job involved so much more than answering phones and letters, I became more entrenched at work and was soon invited to join brainstorming meetings. Better still, I was able to hitch a ride to work with a new hire who was too sluggish in the morning to even consider eating carrots.

Nina Hagen and Lene Lovich.

CHAPTER 6

All the Rage

The "Me" decade was summed up in 1985 by a singer from Detroit who found fame, fortune, and furs, proclaiming, "We're living in a material world and I am a material girl." That same year, for those seeking an antidote to sugarcoated self-indulgence, there was *Meat Is Murder* by the Smiths, an introspective album that entered the British charts at #1 and went gold in the States and much of the Western world. The very month I was hired at PETA, the morose and melodic Smiths embarked on their first U.S. tour. Like legions of other unhinged youth disenchanted with pop culture, my friends and I looked forward to the upcoming concert like pyromaniacs anticipating the Fourth of July.

Ingrid, to show her support for the new vegetarian superheroes, bought balcony seats for all ten PETA staffers, though I already had plans to sit up close with a college chum, Patti, who listened to the Smiths nonstop in her messy dorm room. Patti was a short and shapely Latina, with dark blond shoulder-length hair, thick and tidy makeup, and a slight, endearing Castilian lisp that would have led to many a fat lip had she been a he. The sold-out show was at the elegant Warner Theater, steps away from the White House, and the crowd wore black.

Meat Is Murder wasn't just the title of the album, but also the haunting closing track, in which Morrissey, the singer and songwriter, croons, "The flesh you so fancifully fry is death for no reason and death for no reason is murder." After pushing this view for years, only to have most people turn away, my spiky white hair stood even more on end as I watched thousands hang on every word when the band performed the provocative song live.

At the time, the animal rights movement was still largely considered a quaint concern associated more with Doris Day than rock stars. Morrissey became a bona fide folk hero to vegetarians, as Helen Reddy did to feminists when she released "I Am Woman" or Sir Mix-a-Lot did to women with big butts when he recorded "Baby Got Back." Because of the Smiths' massive young following, Morrissey also made animal rights suddenly relevant among the student set. To try and make use of this, I smuggled a camera inside and shot black-and-white pictures for the Student Action Corps for Animals newsletter, which was handed out on campuses across the country. Having the Smiths on the cover meant that kids would snap it up rather than rip it up. I also tried to get an interview with Morrissey, but was told by the concert promoter, "Dream on—he won't even talk to *Rolling Stone.*"

As the spirited concert came to a close, Patti and I dashed outside to the stage door to make one last attempt to snag an interview. The backstage guard, busy fending off a herd of gothic groupies, wasn't interested in passing my request on to the band. It seemed futile, but I waited earnestly. Meanwhile, Patti slyly slipped away from the throng and worked her ample charms on a crew member near the tour bus. After just a few minutes she was back—with a devious smile.

"I'm going back to the hotel with a roadie," she whispered with a wink. "I'll get Morrissey's room number somehow and call you."

While my other friends carried on for cocktails to the dank old 930 Club on F Street, I scurried to my hot and musty one-room dwelling on S Street and sat by the open window waiting for the phone to ring. After two sweaty hours, when I had almost given up hope, the call came.

"Shoreham Hotel, Room 716," Patti lisped quietly. "That's it, I gotta go."

I nervously phoned the hotel and, to my surprise, was put through to the room.

"Hello?" Morrissey yawned, half asleep.

"Hi," I said, struggling to deepen my overanxious twenty-year-old voice. "Sorry if I woke you up, but this is the only way I could get through. I'd like to ask a few questions for an animal rights magazine. It's hard for us to get people's attention, and you're the biggest lure we've ever had."

I fully expected to hear the phone slam down. Instead, Morrissey yawned again.

"Oh, sure," he said, seeming to rise and shine a bit. "Most interviews are so tiresome, especially on tour," he said matter-of-factly. "But since this is for the animals, obviously I'm duty-bound."

"Thanks," I said, relieved, my head cocked into my shoulder to keep the phone in place while I shakily gripped a pen and pad of paper. "How did this all come about—what made you an animal person?"

"I always thought animals were very much like children," he replied. "They look to us to help them and protect them. If you love animals, obviously it doesn't make sense to hurt them, much less eat them. I became a vegetarian when I was eleven or twelve, growing up in Manchester, and my mother was a staunch vegetarian as long as I can remember. She goes on antihunt rallies and has influenced me very much. We were very poor, and I thought that meat was a good source of nutrition. Then I learned the truth. I guess you could say I repent for those years now. Yuck. Eating meat is the most disgusting thing I can think of. It's chewing up decaying flesh. It's like biting into your grandmother."

I laughed while busily taking notes and fumbled on to the next question.

"Tell some of the ups and downs of calling your album *Meat Is Murder*."

"As soon as we decided on that as the title track, it made headlines," he said. "It's a very simple statement, but often simple statements can become incredibly effective. Nobody seems to be saying anything meaningful in pop music. We got an overwhelmingly positive response, although we did one show in Stoke and somebody threw sausages onto the stage and they hit me in the face and got in my mouth. I had to run off and heave—I really vomited. But that was an isolated case. When we played in Madrid, we did an open-air concert in front of 350,000 people, and it was televised to all of Spain. During 'Meat Is Murder,' they translated the words on the screen, which was very gratifying, especially in such a meaty country. I get mail every day from people all over saying how glad they are that someone is finally saying this, and that they've taken the death out of their diet."

"What do you think of those who might see the show, and even sing along, but have a hamburger afterward?" I asked sheepishly.

"At least they've had to think about it. Lots of people are open to change, but others are very influenced by the people around them, and many are stuck with carnivores. Also, people feel threatened because they think you are asking them to change their entire lifestyle. I say to those people that they should try gradually, that it's not absolutely changing your identity. Once you have an intelligent debate with somebody, you can see their edges soften. The whole idea of vegetarianism is so basic, it's much healthier, and I think everybody knows that. Nobody can come up with a good argument for eating animals. People say, 'Well, it's tasty'—but it's only tasty once you season it and cook it and you have to do three hundred things to it to disguise its true taste. If you did that to a piece of fabric, it would probably taste quite nice."

"This is all great," I said, wishing I knew shorthand. "Any closing thoughts for our easily distracted student readers? This is probably the only edition of this newsletter they'll ever look at."

"Just please don't kill anything. These are pathetically basic words, but get through your life without killing and making animals pay for your pleasures—they're mostly trivial pleasures—it's not anything that anybody really needs. We were all raised with the concept that animals are there to be used, but they're not. It's just those dreadful industries that do it."

We carried on kibitzing about food, roadkill, and music, then he asked a few questions of me.

"I'm fresh out of college," I explained. "I've volunteered for animal groups since high school, and I just started working full-time for PETA—People for the Ethical Treatment of Animals." He hadn't heard of us yet.

"We do all sorts of campaigns, though our forté is undercover investigations, not just in slaughterhouses, but in labs, fur farms, circuses . . . we're not just against meat—we're against everything!" I yelped.

"Me, too," he said, dryly. "If there's ever anything I can do to help, please don't hesitate to ask."

After we exchanged addresses, I told him how much Siouxsie and the Banshees' antifur song "Skin" had impressed me five years before, and that I hoped it wasn't another five years before another pro-animal song came around.

"Listen to 'Assault & Battery' by Howard Jones and 'No Meat' by Captain Sensible," he advised.

"Definitely," I said. "I wish there was an album to bring all these songs together."

"There's an idea," Morrissey replied. "We have a live version of 'Meat Is Murder' which hasn't been released yet, if you're interested . . ."

Thus, haphazardly, began my career working with artists: no professional connections, no inside track, just good old-fashioned Pussy Power, per Patti, and a bit of the gift of gab. I wet my hair in the bathroom sink to cool off, as I often did in that un-air-conditioned abode on hot summer nights, then unfurled my foam sofa bed and floated to sleep, feeling inspired.

Wax Trax Records was both a store and a music label in Chicago. The store, a midwestern punk institution in the 1980s, was colossal, with fetish wear, offensive T-shirts, and Crazy Color hair dye in addition to every trendy album and single from around the world. I stopped in once at sixteen, while making my way across the country on a Greyhound bus, and it was the only time I ever regretted having promised my parents I'd quit shoplifting. The label, which had offices above the store, released hardcore dance music by artists such as Divine, Front 242, 1000 Homo DJs, and the Revolting Cocks. I don't think any of their songs were ever licensed to Disney films. Wax Trax's biggest band was Ministry, the pioneers of industrial and techno music, whose breakthrough hit was called "Everyday Is Halloween."

"These look like your kind of people," said Linda from PETA's mailroom as she plopped a package from Wax Trax onto my desk. Inside were a bunch of records and a letter from Al Jourgensen of Ministry seeking permission to use an audio snippet from our vivisection video for a nightmarish dance tune he was producing.

I phoned Wax Trax and was passed to Jim Nash, who owned both the store and the label.

"Good news," I said. "We don't copyright—you can use the laboratory bit, no problem, but we'd like to draft something for the liner notes about animal experimentation."

"Great!" Jim hollered. "And congratulations on closing those fuckers down. We saw it on the news. But my niece still wants to kill them."

"You know, it's funny you guys got in touch just now," I confided. "We're developing an album but haven't figured out a label yet."

"Cool. What bands have you got?"

"Honestly, right now it's just the Smiths," I said modestly. "But we're looking at Siouxsie and the Banshees, Wall of Voodoo, Talk Talk, and others who have animal-related songs."

"*Just* the Smiths? When can you come to Chicago?!"

The next Friday, Ingrid had her assistant fill in for me at the reception desk, and I was happily off on my first business trip.

I've loved flying ever since I was a tyke, when I climbed aboard an Air California flight with my dad to go a cousin's bas mitzvah in San Jose. I always request the emergency exit row—not just because I'm six-five and need the extra room, but so that I can be Shoe Monitor. You see, when a plane crash-lands and the inflatable slide pops out, one of your exit-row duties is to make sure that the ladies remove their high heels so they don't puncture the slide and ruin every-body's escape. Though I have an impulsive side, I'm very coolheaded in a crisis. My last words might be "Off with those pumps!" but I'll have died a hero. Sometimes I'm denied the exit row for remarking at the check-in counter that I'd allow whoever ordered a vegetarian meal to escape first and make any fur wearers go to the end of the line.

I arrived safely in Chicago and stayed with Jim Nash and his brawny copper-topped boyfriend, Danny, in their shad-owy loft across the alley behind Wax Trax. I slept on a long leather sofa; fortunately, my gracious hosts had sheets thick enough to mask the smell. We held our business meeting over beers at a dimly lit dive called the Orbit Room.

"It's great to use these songs that are already out, as a base," Jim reasoned, "but if you really want people to pay attention to this album, we have to get new material, too, hopefully from someone significant."

"I'm sure we could," I replied, ever optimistic. "I don't know who, but we can cast about . . . as long as it isn't any-body too preachy."

"Exactly, they have to be the kind of lunatic artist that would fit on Wax Trax," Jim said. "We're a small label with a twisted little niche, and we wouldn't do well with a country group or a jazz combo . . . unless maybe they were fronted by someone with a speech impediment."

We were joined by a black-haired teenage beauty named Julia (Jim's daughter from a previous sexuality) and his screwball niece, Liz, both of whom worked at Wax Trax, Julia in the store and Liz at the label.

"Good!" Jim exclaimed, pouring Julia some beer. "Now Dan isn't the only underage drinker."

"A lot of our roster would do this album" offered Liz, between drags on a cigarette, in her droning, nasal voice, which always sounds mocking—and often is. "I bet we can get the synth bands like Attrition and Chris & Cosey, and Jim knows Shriekback."

As Liz blew smoke away from the table, she was thunderstruck with an idea.

"What about Zamfir and his magic pan flute from those overnight TV ads?!"

"My dream person for this would be Nina Hagen." I sighed.

"It doesn't get more lunatic than that," Jim laughed. "Let's all just put out some feelers—I know we'll pull this together." Jim and I shook on the deal, and then we all went back to the loft to watch *Desperate Living.*

Nina Hagen is one of the most peculiar artists of the twentieth century: her story involves Cold War intrigue, yodeling, punk, and pot. She grew up in gloomy East Berlin in the 1960s and '70s, when Soviet soldiers shot anyone trying to flee over the wall or dash through Checkpoint Charlie. Her mother was an opera star and her stepfather a concert pianist, both very famous throughout the Eastern bloc. Nina was classically trained from an early age to follow in her mother's operatic tradition, but she much preferred Janis

Joplin and the other outlawed rock that floated over on air-waves from West Berlin. In 1976, her stepfather was allowed into West Germany for a high-profile concert appearance, during which he criticized the Communist regime—which instantly branded him a dissident and barred his return. In the ensuing controversy, Nina and her mother were also booted out of their homeland.

Once over the Wall, Nina was sought after by record companies scrambling to capitalize on her notoriety as well as her surprising vocal range and raucous sensuality. She signed with Columbia, but instead of recording an album of romantic Schlager tunes, Nina developed her sound and style in the burgeoning punk scene in London, where she lived with an all-girl band called the Slits. In 1978, Nina released her debut album, with songs about people getting so fat in front of the TV they explode, the friendly lesbian hookers in the Berlin train station, and her unwavering love of the big city. In the surreal closing ballad, "Naturträne," Nina sings about flinging open her window to gleefully inhale the filthy city air, trilling the lyrics in her soaring soprano but closing each verse with gagging sounds.

The record company wasn't sure it had made a wise investment, but soon after its release Nina Hagen's debut was #1 in Germany and one of the top sellers of the year through-out Europe. A successful follow-up featured a single called "African Reggae," in which Nina yodels about marijuana; it became a worldwide dance hit, so she moved to Hollywood to launch her career in America. That's when I first met her.

It would be misleading to say I was a "friend" of Nina's back then—"stalker" might be more appropriate. In any case, from the time my punk pal Connie and I first heard Nina on Rodney Bingenheimer's Sunday night program on KROQ, she became our favorite performer, and we never missed a show. Many of the clubs she first appeared in were so tiny that there often wasn't really a backstage, so it was easy to say hello. At one such gig I brought her a fluorescent polka-dotted rain bonnet I had found in a thrift shop, and we rambled about the latest obsession working its way into her songs: UFOs. I shared with her my obsession with animal rights.

"Any chance you're a vegetarian?" I asked.

"No . . . not really," she replied bashfully in her cartoon-like squeak.

"You mean 'No . . . not yet?' " I said playfully.

It was exciting to watch Nina become a cult figure in America, with sold-out tours and amusing appearances on programs like *Late Night with David Letterman* and *Merv Griffin*. Merv was particularly smitten with her—though I can't imagine what his mature, blue-haired viewers thought when pink-haired Nina held one of her shiny black stilettos to her ear like a phone and started talking to herself using several of her otherworldly voices.

An eccentric like Nina Hagen may not be the sort of star most new charities would pursue to help establish a public image, but I couldn't help myself. As soon as we signed the deal with Wax Trax, Nina was among the first artists I approached about writing a song for PETA. In between answering phones and letters at the reception desk, I eagerly prepared packages for bands, blindly mailing them via management and crossing my fingers.

A good number of the packages ended up in the trash, as many music industry people hadn't yet heard of PETA or didn't want their artists associated with agitators like us. Some bands wanted to participate, but their wary record companies wouldn't allow it. With the Smiths as bait, we did acquire most of the previously released songs we aimed for, as well as some specially recorded songs by Wax Trax bands, but we were in dire need of a catchy new tune to be the centerpiece.

Late one evening, as I was switching off the lights at work, the phone rang.

"Hallooo, Dan Mathews pleeease," said the caller in a guttural voice reminiscent of the demon in *The Exorcist*. I thought it was a friend pulling a prank, but the static and hiss on the line suggested it was an overseas call.

"Uh . . . yes, this is Dan," I said tepidly.

"Danimal!" squealed the voice, suddenly high-pitched, chased by what sounded like a little girl's cackle. It was Nina calling from London. She had received the PETA package and was already writing a song for us, called "Don't Kill the Animals." It would be a duet, she explained, with her friend Lene Lovich, a similarly strange singer known for the arty club hits "Lucky Number" and "New Toy." She also told me she had become a vegetarian.

"Don't Kill the Animals" is a chirpy anthem, with Nina and Lene sounding like cheerleaders on helium, rapping lines like "Life is for living, the animals agree, if they were meant to be eaten, they'd be growing on trees." Well before the album's release, the song began serving as PETA's calling card. I gave a tape to Morrissey when the Smiths came back for a second tour of America, and he loved it so much that he had it played throughout the concert halls just before the band took the stage each night, creating an incredible buzz among the exact crowd we needed to peddle our record to. Nina drew both chuckles and applause when she previewed the song to Middle America on yet another *Merv Griffin* appearance.

I began crisscrossing the country on weekends, glad-handing nightclub DJs with an advance cassette and visiting edgy rock stations. I was booked for lengthy interviews in which I would play songs from the forthcoming album and bring up local practices such as the gruesome electro-ejaculation breeding procedure used by primate laboratories in Boston and Atlanta, and common meat-trade mutilations at the stockyards in Fort Worth. In Chicago, I informed listeners that Holocaust survivor Isaac Bashevis Singer was inspired to write the famous line, "To animals, all people are Nazis," after watching workers prod panicking cows up the ramp at a Chicago slaughterhouse. It was around this time that Ingrid told me to stop answering the phones and move into the newly formed campaigns department, where I could work on the project full-time.

We put the album together in London, where we also planned overseas promotions (RCA bought the rights to "Don't Kill the Animals" for Europe, where it actually hit the pop charts). During my downtime, I'd gawk at the ruins of the Battersea Power Plant, enjoy the latest display at the campy London Dungeon torture museum, or go on the guided Jack the Ripper walk just after dark.

One night during my stay, Nina called with a spur-of-the-moment dinner invitation, promising a surprise guest. As the cab pulled up to her Lurline Gardens apartment, I imagined the person to be someone who channels past lives, or a Hare Krishna she'd met on the Tube. I was wrong.

"You must be the animal nut Nina keeps yapping about," said the redheaded man with a cynical scowl as he opened the door. "She's in the kitchen baking an eggless cake that she insists won't taste like shit." It was Johnny Rotten, of the Sex Pistols, who Nina had kept in touch with since her first foray into London years before. We sat on the couch, and he pointed to some cans of beer on the table, his delicate way of offering me one. I always treasured the sarcasm in his songs and interviews, and although I felt a bit anxious, I was ecstatic to be the target of it in person, especially at Nina's place. It was the punk equivalent of walking into a dinner party at JoAnn Worley's house and being called a "hockey puck" by Don Rickles.

"Just so you leave me alone, these Dalmatian shoes I'm wearing aren't real Dalmatian, they're just leather made to look spotty." Considering the source, I half wished he had told me that they were real Dalmatian and that he'd skinned the dog himself. Oh, well. Finally, Nina traipsed in from the kitchen, kissed me hello, and set down a giant bowl of tofu wurstel with sauerkraut.

"It's the future food of the astronaut!" she exclaimed.

Nina had just returned from Germany, where she performed classic Brecht and Weill tunes backed by a full orchestra for a TV special, which she showed us on tape while we ate. At the concert, she was projected onto a giant screen in front of the formal audience, but her enormous yellow wig took up most of the frame. After dinner, we discussed the London launch for the PETA album, which Nina was set to host with Lene Lovich at the Limelight, a Gothic church that had been turned into a nightclub.

Upon its release, our little underground record, which we called *Animal Liberation,* was the *New York Times'* Rock Album of the Week and heralded on CNN and MTV, which actually played our amateurish "Don't Kill the Animals" video on a late-night program. Most exciting was reading the weekly nightclub playlists; the song became a staple at Palladium in Manhattan, DV8 in San Francisco, Weekends in Atlanta, and many, many other hotspots.

To more thoroughly align the organization with the song, it seemed logical to ask some of these clubs to have PETA parties—which Lene Lovich bravely agreed to fly over from England to host, free of charge. I say bravely because I barely knew what I was doing; I simply called the clubs' managers—almost all of them complete strangers—and asked if they'd put us up and put out literature in exchange for Lene singing a song or two. I also suggested they cast about for local talent to make the event more of a "happening." Easygoing Lene hopped off the plane and into my rental car with no questions asked, and we embarked on a nationwide tour, often driving with little or no sleep and doing whatever press the clubs drummed up for us.

Lene looks like a rag doll in Kabuki makeup, and has the calm intellect of an ancient soul. She is one of the most articulate people I've ever known, making her points not by restating dull facts and figures but by conjuring up unforgettable images. I learned a great deal listening to her merrily tell reporters things like "For a while I craved the texture of meat, but soon found many things to eat with the same wonderful flesh-ripping sensation." We expected to talk mostly to the alternative weeklies, but ended up in the big daily papers and even on TV.

In some places, like Tulsa, there was no stage, so Lene had to sing and prance around on a grungy bar, careful not to kick over someone's cocktail with her pointy pleather boots. In Chicago, Ministry joined the bill, and the event was transformed into a major PETA benefit. For the New Orleans gig, Lene and I were put up in a remote mansion where our generous but eerie host told us he loved to fly his crop duster on LSD, and repeatedly warned us not to venture into his "basement of the living dead." He placed us in rooms at opposite ends of the old house, but we were sufficiently terrified to creep across the floorboards and huddle in bed together. We didn't really sleep; we just stared at the antique ceiling fan above us, certain that it would descend and decapitate us. The most spectacular night of the tour was in Texas at the ultrachic Starck Club, where dancers from the Dallas Ballet, wearing ski masks and using flashlights as props, performed an elaborately choreographed laboratory break-in to "Don't Kill the Animals" as Lene sang it to the capacity crowd.

"All the scenesters went to Payless to get nonleather shoes for this event," revealed one stylish Texan who attended. This was Todd Oldham, a local designer preparing for the big move to New York, where he would help establish PETA in the fashion world. Another reveler was Marguerite Gordon, a maverick arts patron from Santa Fe who would commission PETA's most imaginative and disturbing traveling displays.

In the wake of the album's success, we enticed many of its artists—along with more mainstream acts like the B-52s and Natalie Merchant—to play an Animal Rights Music Festival on the grounds of the Washington Monument. We hoped to attract 10,000 people and make PETA a cultural force in the nation's capital, especially among the huge student population and influential Capitol Hill staffers and interns; 35,000 showed up, and MTV rotated its first in-depth news piece on our mushrooming cause. Work soon began on a follow-up album called *Tame Yourself,* a much slicker package with Erasure, Belinda Carlisle, Michael Stipe, the Indigo Girls, Jane Wiedlin, and the Pretenders. Besides soliciting their songs, we were able to get many artists involved in campaigns, including k d. lang, who filmed a "Meat Stinks" commercial that got her banned on country radio but caused her album sales to surge (the gold record still hangs behind my desk), and Björk, who posed for PETA's cruelty-free fashion spread in *Spin*.

By the end of the 1980s, "animal rights" was transformed from a grandmotherly concern into a vibrant youth movement freshly embedded on the world's pop-culture radar, as visible in celebrity columns as on the news page. The article that gave us the biggest laugh, as we unpacked boxes in the drafty warehouse that served as our new, much larger headquarters in Kensington, Maryland, came from London, where *Time Out* dubbed PETA "so hip it hurts."

With David in Tucumcari.

CHAPTER 7

DOOFNAC XEMI

Sometimes on the road, on a day off, someone will suggest going to a museum or a mall. For my stock response, I bring up the thoughtful words of the dead stripper/poet Wendy O. Williams: "I don't like art, and I don't like fashion—blowing up expensive things makes me cum." Of course, it's probably just the airs of the art world and the crowds in shopping centers that I hate, because if I'm asked to go thrift shopping, where one can find fascinating paintings and one-of-a-kind fashions, I get all excited.

You can imagine my glee when my best friend, David Cohen, phoned to say that his love affair in L.A. had fizzled and left him without a penny or a possession, and that he wanted me to help him drive back to Washington, stopping in junk stores all along the way so that he'd have knick-knacks for a new apartment. It took all of the self-control I could muster to first offer sympathy for David's broken heart before demanding to know when our road trip would begin.

For me and David and other thrift enthusiasts, second-hand shops are like magical, grimy time machines. When you walk through the door, you never know how far back you'll be transported, or how far out. You can peruse high school yearbooks from the 1940s in which the withered world of a stranger is revealed in notes scribbled by classmates alongside their black-and-white pictures. It's fun to guess who was the slut, who was gay, and who became governor. Sometimes it's all the same person.

I like a junk shop's record section best of all. There are dusty vinyl albums from the 1950s that teach you how to converse more colorfully at parties, or to contort your face in exercises designed to get rid of double chins, or to clog dance. I found one groovy record called *Plantasia*, an ethereal easy-listening album that is supposed to soothe your houseplants into growing healthier and heartier. I swear it worked on my daisies. And they're plastic. Number one on my thrift hit parade is a 1970s Moog synthesizer rendition of Johnny Cash's "I Walk the Line," sung by what sounds like a throat cancer patient holding one of those magic microphones to the surgical patch on his Adam's apple.

Thrift stores offer clothes to suit almost any taste, as long as it's bad. David once scored a pair of overalls emblazoned with the *Hee Haw* logo, and I got a rubber motorcycle jacket that looks too much like leather but cost only $5. Most people draw the line at used underwear, but not us. David has a collection of secondhand military long johns, and I wear some dead man's oversize skivvies as short pants. We would never, however, be so vile as to buy a used pan, as it may have been used to cook meat.

I learned to scavenge others' discards from my mother, who, when I was in ninth grade, found me a pair of size-twelve pumps at Goodwill to wear to *Rocky Horror*. Mom, by now in her sixties, had moved to Arizona, where she worked at the courthouse in Scottsdale. Neither David nor I had seen her for some time, so we looked forward to staying with her on the first night of our journey.

Mom had just changed her name to Perry Lawrence. She loved the idea of having a unisex moniker and had written me that she was considering "Perry Lawrence," so I replied with a postcard addressed to that name to see if it felt comfortable to her. It felt great, so she took the postcard to the DMV as proof-of-self, and they issued her a new driver's license. As always, she posed for the picture like she had just won an election, her pink lips beaming a smile and her baby blue eyes popping out.

"As you can see, I decided to let my hair go white," she said, flipping her bob teasingly as we walked into a Mexican restaurant. "I finally thought, *fuck it*."

We ordered guacamole, veggie fajitas, and margaritas, and Perry lamented her increased hearing problems. She also complained about how dreary fellow seniors can be. Scanning an elderly couple shuffling their way to the cash register, she announced, "This is my peer group now—please shoot me."

"So, David darling, tell me what happened in L.A.?" Perry asked over the mariachi music, sliding around in the booth so that she was directly opposite him in order to read his lips.

"I fell in love with a tattooed ex-Mormon artist in Silverlake when I was out visiting friends," he said. "I moved in with him, but after a month I was ready to move out. I like the seasons and the gardening climate back East." David is primarily a loner and a landscaper, who, when I first met him at American University, resembled the young, playful Mel Gibson, before Mel got that crazy born-again look in his eye. And before David started shaving his head. By now he had his trademark look of a fit and friendly skinhead.

As we left the restaurant, thinking nobody was watching,

Perry nonchalantly burrowed her finely manicured finger-nails into the free mint bowl and grabbed a handful so that David and I had a stash for the trip. Cool as always, without even looking down, mom quietly released the hard candies into her purse. Only her purse wasn't open. The mints scattered all over the tile floor, sounding like hailstones to everyone except for deaf Perry. The Mexican manager suddenly appeared, with a puzzled look on his face, but Mom just kept strutting, oblivious, and coyly whispered to us, "I've got a little surprise for you. . . ."

We carried on to a grubby desert honky-tonk, where it happened to be karaoke night—which I despise—but to lift David's spirits, I told him I'd sing any song he wanted. He made me get up in front of the bikers and sing Dolly Parton's "Here You Come Again." I couldn't find my key, which made the experience all the more humiliating. Mom buried her face in her hands, but David, in fits of laughter, simply turned his chair around so that all I could see was the back of his wobbling bald head, which looked like a spastic baby's butt.

The next morning, with the Hallmark family moment behind us, David and I eagerly embarked on our epic thrift shop excursion. We decided to shun the big city Salvation Army stores in favor of the less-picked-over small-town boutiques, such as Janet's Indoor Yard Sale in Wickenburg, Charlene's Treasure Chest in Fort Smith, and, of course, the little shops run by the Association for Retarded Citizens. We'd simply pull off the freeway in Anytown, USA, and consult the local phone book. The most intriguing and bountiful place of all, however, we stumbled upon by accident.

We were cruising through the cold, rural flat desert of New Mexico, not far from the Texas border, and pulled off to get some gas. As we ambled along looking for a coffee shop, we found ourselves in a largely forsaken ghost town called Tucumcari. It's one of those cities that boomed when Route 66 started bringing every car down Main Street in the 1930s, then went bust when the speedy interstates drained away the traffic in the '70s. Tumbleweeds blew along the cracked sidewalk. The old movie palace, in ruins, was playing a feature titled *Closed.* An old beauty salon seemed to be hanging on by a hair.

Then we saw it, like a desert mirage, the big sign mesmerizing us from overhead: DOOFNAC XEMI. A smaller sign read THINGS. It was a restaurant that had gone under and been turned into a secondhand store that appeared to contain the discards of every citizen who had abandoned the town. And it was open.

"Oh, my God," gasped David as he brought his green station wagon to a screeching halt in the empty parking lot. "I think we've hit the mother lode." We ran for the door like a couple of New Jersey Jews at a midnight madness sale at the Price Club. The overstuffed orange booths that had once seated hungry travelers now held scads of Class A trash from yesteryear, and the perky fake wood hostess station was now staffed by a weary old man. He sat motionless on a stool next to an AM radio tuned to a classic country station.

Our usual plan of attack consists of David rummaging through housewares and clothes while I tackle books and records, but here everything was piled together, so we just went to opposite ends and worked our way to the middle. We'd holler each other's name from behind some smelly stack, and a hand would shoot up holding some amazing artifact for the other's perusal. There was a lot of hollering.

We found sexual revolution greeting cards with slogans like "Help Stop Rape . . . Say Yes," a Day-Glo velvet poster of a curvy black girl with a giant Afro called "Chocolate Fantasy," and a cardboard pop-out fireplace, complete with a swirling red flamelike lamp, which David would set up in every motel room for the remainder of the trip. We found paperback serializations of *That Girl* and *Get Smart,* a mint-quality hardback of *Valley of the Dolls*, and the *Good Housekeeping Guide to Refrigerator Desserts*—perfect inaugural volumes for any bookcase. Plus it'd be a cinch for dairy-wary David to use soy milk and turn the recipes into kosher vegan delights when his parents, Harris and Yetta, visited over Hanukkah.

I came upon a stack of classic disco records, with show tunes and vintage Barbra Streisand mixed in, so I said a little silent prayer for the AIDS casualty that had likely left this vinyl mess behind. At first I thought it might have belonged to someone who'd merely upgraded his collection to CDs, but then reasoned that only death would come between most Barbra freaks and those posterlike foldout record jackets. At the bottom of the pile was an album called *Co-Star with Tallulah Bankhead,* which came with a script so that you could read scenes alongside Tallulah's gravelly voice. When I play it loudly, the neighbors simply think I have a batty aunt visiting.

David found a singing Suzy Moppet doll with wide eyes, freckles, yellow yarn pigtails, and a red Sunday dress. When you push her tummy, she shrieks, in Tammy Faye Bakker's baby voice, "Jesus takes a frown and turns it upside down!" Nearby was a stack of "God Bless Our Trailer" salad plates, with nary a chip. Among the framed art was a painting that had as its background a line of perfectly poised ballerinas, who are overtaken in the foreground by a perplexed, clumsy clown. Beneath the sad jester was a small inscription: "Then I realized I was different from the others."

Just when we thought we were through, David spotted a not-too-filthy wiglet, which he hung snugly from the back of his baseball cap to create the impression of a truly realistic mullet.

"This should land me some dates when we drive through Oklahoma," he said.

It took us a good while to weed our hastily snatched items into "must have" and "can do without" piles. The quiet old man, who ignored our fanatical ramblings, loaded our precious artifacts into the battered grocery bags he kept behind the counter.

"You've got an amazing place here," I said, "but what does 'Doofnac Xemi' mean?"

"Well," he responded slowly, "when I bought this place, the sign said 'Mexican Food.' I just rearranged the letters."

We lugged our haul to the car, and the old man obliged in taking our picture in front of his store and then waved good-bye as we took off down old Route 66.

Crossing into the Texas panhandle at dusk, I eagerly sifted through the box of stupid greeting cards and found two that summed up our sentiments so well we displayed them on the dashboard: "So Sorry About Your Divorce . . . Now Let's Party!" and "Help Fight the War on Poverty . . . Buy Me Things."

PETA's surprise party for Calvin Klein.

CHAPTER 8

This Is a Raid

I don't want people to go over the edge, but if they do, it might as well be documented, and I pray that someone will send me the article. I have quite a collection. Some of the highlights include stories about a man jailed for beating his wife because she didn't have enough Christmas spirit; a man who leaped from a speeding car to grab his cigarette, which had blown out of the window; and a woman who gave birth on the subway in front of rush-hour commuters—and acted like nothing was happening. It doesn't count if it's a parody in the *Weekly World News* or the *Onion;* it has to have really happened and been covered by a normal newspaper. My bulletin board, filled with such cuttings, is the envy of the office. Well, some of the office. All right, just me and a few other crackpots.

Alas, when I moved into PETA's campaigns department in the late 1980s, most of the weird clippings sent my way were not things I wanted to glibly pin on the wall. One article involved an enterprising businessman in Oklahoma who proposed building a rabbit plant. Here, bunnies would not simply be butchered for their fur and meat, but for an added profit, their frantic screams would be recorded and marketed as cassettes to hunters, who could play the blood-curdling tapes in the woods to attract predator animals that they could then more lazily shoot. *Good times.* Fortunately, the proposal violated zoning laws, and construction was blocked.

One fine day, just after I had been put in charge of PETA's antifur campaign, someone sent me a more useful story. It was a page torn from *Vogue* about designers who use fur, their bold names circled in red ink and "Get 'em" scribbled in the margin. The suggestion had potential, so I pinned the frayed cutting to the wall beside my desk for inspiration. As the fight against fur in the 1970s and '80s had largely involved often futile attempts to ban leghold traps or to pressure monolithic department store chains to stop selling fur, it seemed that shifting the focus to high-profile designers would be a terrific way to update the debate and energize the issue. A personal target, especially someone famous, is much more exciting than a faceless corporate target. Pursuing this strategy also meant that I could spend more time in my favorite city: New York.

I often ventured by train from D.C. to New York for fund-raising meetings or demonstrations—occasionally ending up in jail, though more often bunking with PETA sympathizers. As Manhattan hotel prices aren't conducive to nonprofit budgets, I stayed at first with phone friends I had made while manning the reception desk. This included a short, stout, amicable Italian senior named Yolanda, who had Coke-bottle glasses and straight salt-and-pepper hair, and who was always calling for more PETA literature to place on the card table she'd set up in the West Village on weekends.

"I've got plenty of room!" she'd crow. "You're always welcome!"

I arrived carrying my mustard-colored secondhand Samsonite to find that she lived in a small windowless interior studio, on Sheridan Square. Chatty Yolanda cooked us a pasta dinner, then nonchalantly put on her nightgown and pulled out a little hide-a-bed for us to share. It was a multi-generational slumber party; we conked out only after we had talked about everything from how to pronounce the word *vivisection* to our favorite World War II movies. Perhaps inspired by circumstance, I chose *Harold and Maude*, which qualifies because Ruth Gordon's character has a concentration camp tattoo. Wonderful as Yolanda was, I decided to look around and see what other cost-conscious sleeping arrangements a gregarious fellow in his twenties might uncover in New York City.

The next bed was more comfortable—it belonged to a soft-spoken, buff young architect I met at an East Village club called the Pyramid, who supplemented his income by modeling. He had a tidy place on the Upper West Side where I stayed during a few early forays into the city. But before long, he met someone else—a local—and moved in with him. Oh, well, I'll always have the memories . . . and the *Esquire* fitness issue with him on the cover.

Finally, my flamboyant ex-roommate from Rome, Michael Filippis, came to New York to be a party promoter and a DJ, crimping his bleached hair and adopting the nickname Goldy Loxxx. Goldy moved into a huge loft on Chambers Street. It had a large walk-in closet, which he offered to me as a perpetual crash pad. I wasn't the only stray cat in the loft: there was also Birdy, a big calico who charged the front door and ferociously attacked the ankles of anyone who dared enter, and Jesse, a smaller, sweeter tabby. They were the real fur that kept me warm on the purple fake fur bathrobe that served as my mattress on the closet's hardwood floor.

This closet, which I also shared with Goldy's flashy club clothes, became my Big Apple base. When the *Philadelphia Inquirer* did a story on PETA's feisty but frugal Manhattan high jinks, they had a photographer get shots of me rising and shining for a day of activism in my cozy little Tribeca tomb amid the fluorescent jumpsuits and velvet trousers. It was from this unlikely headquarters that I embarked on PETA's first major fashion offensive.

At the time, the most mainstream name in fur was Calvin Klein, who had been designing an annual fur coat collection since Carter was president. I set my sights on Calvin not just because he was America's most successful designer, but because I thought he might be the most sensible; he didn't seem as pompous, arrogant, haughty, indifferent, and self-centered as the other designers. I could actually imagine us being friends. Yet Calvin, like the other designers trumpeted in that *Vogue* article, never responded to our earnest appeals sent by mail. I imagine that the videos of squirming minks being injected with weed killer and panic-stricken foxes being anally electrocuted never reached the actual people who, without thinking much about it, envision clever ways to turn the decomposing, chemically treated remains of these animals into expensive accessories. Rather, I bet these videos were deemed a nuisance and tossed into the trash. Follow-up calls to each hectic office invariably met the same response: "If you sent it, we got it, if there's interest, we'll call you."

What did we have to do in order to find fifteen minutes on a designer's agenda?

I proposed to Ingrid that we show up en masse at Calvin's office and refuse to leave until he renounced fur. We weren't sure that Calvin would comply, but we figured an occupation would make all our targets realize that if they ignore the reasonable concerns of a peaceful group plodding along outside department stores, they might face an angry mob in their office. Upon further discussion, we reasoned that since we'd quickly be tossed out, we should leave a calling card, such as stickers on the walls and leaflets on desks. One thing led to another, and we were soon mapping out a full-scale raid, including bullhorns and paint. Since this was the first volley in our designer initiative, it had to be jarring enough to prompt everyone in the frivolous fashion world to have at least one short, serious thought about the sadistic industry that so many of them gratuitously promote.

The first order of business was to case the place, much like a thief would. To do this, I replaced my de rigueur Krispy Kreme sweatshirt with a snug black turtleneck, slicked my hair back to look more "Seventh Avenue," and walked into the busy foyer of the office building on Thirty-ninth Street that houses Calvin Klein's world headquarters.

"Good morning," I said, moving along past the security desk.

"Good morning to you," the middle-aged guard replied. "Where are you going?"

"Calvin Klein," I said with a strained smile. "I'm an intern. With first-day jitters."

"Tenth floor—and good luck."

Who says New Yorkers aren't friendly?

The elevator doors opened to reveal a small lobby, clean and sleek, much in the style that Calvin is known for. At first glance there was a slight obstacle: the lobby was fully enclosed, and the door leading to the office suites was locked. Fortunately, the reception counter was low enough to hop over. Most promising of all was the large silver Calvin Klein logo embossed on the white wall; we could paint "Kills Animals" in bright red underneath to illustrate our point. By the time the receptionist finished her phone call and looked up to ask who I was there to see, I was gone. But I'd be back in a few days.

The raiding party consisted of a cluster of Manhattan's most spirited animal activists, among them Kat, very chic with short black hair and spit curls; Emily, a tall blonde whose friendly facade masks an alarmingly raucous New Yorker; and Anne, a fifty-something Irish mother with long red hair, an easy smile, and a son who was a Midtown cop. The crucial role of spray-painter went to the steady-handed Lisa Lange, who came up from Washington to join us. Lisa had recently started working at PETA, having been hired by Ingrid in the jail at Pottsville, Pennsylvania, where they were both serving time for disrupting a pigeon shoot.

We faxed a short advisory to a few key news desks stating that members of PETA would occupy a major fur designer's office—we didn't say who—and invited photographers interested in covering our surprise party to meet us at the corner of Thirty-ninth and Eighth at 10 a.m. sharp. A good handful showed up—as well as a few uninvited TV crews that had somehow been tipped off. This made me very, very nervous, as I couldn't imagine finagling the whole lot past security. I already had butterflies in my stomach, and they began flapping their wings.

Now came the hardest part, an acting job considerably more challenging than the silly Fiat commercial I had filmed at Cinecittá.

I led the six well-dressed trespassers into the building like an anxious teacher shepherding students on a field trip,

our posse trailed by a slew of cameras. We were faced, luckily, with the same security guard with whom I had chatted
before. He surveyed the group and rose with a quizzical look
on his face.

"What's going on?" he asked.

"My first assignment—it's a media project!" I chirped
enthusiastically.

"Well, any TV crews will have to get clearance before I
can let them up."

"No problem," I said, forcing a smile. "I'll just bring up
the other interns, and we'll send someone back down for the
TV crews. Come along, everybody."

Before he could react, I prodded all of the protesters—
and the photographer from the Associated Press—down the
hallway and into an elevator that had just opened. Not to be
left behind, the other photographers and crews tried to
elbow past the security desk and get into their own elevator.

"Just a minute, you've got to wait," the guard directed
the group behind us.

"Yeah, well, we didn't come here to sit downstairs and
miss all the action," replied an agitated reporter.

"What action?" The guard instantly cast a suspicious
glare at those of us cramming ourselves into the lift. He realized he'd been duped and angrily started moving toward us.

"I want all of you to wait!" he screamed.

My heart started jack-hammering. I kept a poker face,
but my finger took on a life of its own, alternately pressing
"Close" and "10" so many times, so quickly, that I'm surprised the system didn't short-circuit. We held our breath as
the guard sprinted for the door. I considered having Emily
morph into her Lady Wrestler alter ego and leap out of the
elevator to do a body block.

"*CLOSE*, you fucker!" Emily finally shouted, veins bulging on her fair forehead. Almost as if it were afraid of her, the door slid shut—without a second to spare. The pounding of fists on the outer metal door made us jump, but the sound faded as we began our ascent. I wiped the sweat from my brow and looked around to double-check that all of the principles had made it. We anxiously laughed. Kat bit her perfectly lined crimson lip.

"Looks like I got an exclusive," smirked the AP photographer. Lisa, with a baseball cap slung low over her pretty face and mop of dark hair, pulled a can of spray paint from her jacket and nodded with a slight smile.

The bell rang, the doors opened on ten, and out we exploded like a ferocious pack of Keystone Kops. At first, the group of people innocently waiting in the lobby for an appointment looked up at the unlikely marauders with a simple jolt. Then, as the yelling and painting began, they gasped and looked around in a panic, realizing there was no easy way out. Lisa tidily sprayed "Kills Animals" beneath Calvin's logo while Anne and Emily chanted slogans and spread leaflets all around, leaving them on the little tables and forcing them into the hands of the mortified bystanders as they gathered in a frenzied clump to escape into the next elevator down. Kat, her accomplices, and I ominously approached the refined receptionist. She stared up at us in horror, as if we were the Manson family on a mission.

"Good morning," I said as politely as possible, ever mindful that my middle name is Lee, after the gracious Virginia general. One should strive to be civil even in combat. "We're here to protest Calvin Klein's use of fur, and we'll be taking over your offices until he gives it up." Her jaw dropped. She was too dumbfounded to respond. She just glanced at the vandalism unfolding behind us and slowly backed away from her desk.

"*Someone, call the police!*" she finally shrieked, disappearing into the inner offices.

Sexy Kat, wearing black tights, leaped over the counter like Batgirl and was followed by her cohorts. They prowled through the offices, one of them shouting "Fur pimps!" on the bullhorn, the other plastering stickers on phones and leaving leaflets on desks. You could hear a stampede of expensive shoes scurrying to emergency exits, followed by earsplitting alarm bells. Some workers came out of their offices thinking it was a fire drill, then, bewildered by the pandemonium, locked themselves back inside.

"Where's Calvin?!" Kat forcefully hollered over the din.

"Calvin's not here!" pleaded someone. It was true; he was out at a meeting. But his wife Kelly was there, and security guards, thinking our invasion might be a kidnapping attempt, hustled her quickly and roughly down ten flights of stairs and out of the building.

Meanwhile, back in Calvin's lobby, a distinguished-looking older gentleman burst through the door from the inner offices.

"I don't know *who* you people are, but I demand that you all leave—*now!*" he bellowed.

Rowdy Emily ignored his order but lunged for the open door behind him, and the two of them scuffled right next to the freshly spray-painted wall. It was this thrilling image that the Associated Press ran all over the world that afternoon.

When it was clear that the siege was unfolding pretty much as we'd planned, I took the next elevator down, with the brash notion that I might be able to bring up the rest of the press. As if. The door opened on the ground floor to a swarm of New York's finest, who commandeered the lift and headed up to the tenth floor. Other officers were scattered throughout the foyer, and one of them, unaware that I was involved in the protest, instructed me to leave the building.

Outside, I found all the reporters who hadn't made it upstairs—and others who had been urgently dispatched to the scene—and gave them the lowdown, as well as copies of the video we had sent to Calvin, showing the gory fate of the animals destined for his showroom. Before long, the police descended, escorting the handcuffed protestors into a paddy wagon.

"Make sure you call my son at the Midtown precinct!" Anne shouted at me with a fighting Irish grin. "Maybe we'll get out quicker!" The door was bolted shut, the police van pulled away, and though I was elated that our invasion had succeeded, I wished I had been hauled off with my friends, not so much for the camaraderie but because the people you meet in New York City jails—especially in the Tombs downtown—have absolutely riveting stories to share.

The next morning, at Goldy Loxxx's loft on Chambers Street, I eagerly wiped the sleep from my eyes, gave my purring pillow mates a kiss, came out of the closet, and excitedly read all about PETA's outrageous insurrection in *USA Today*. I felt fairly confident that our high-fashion offensive had been properly launched. I also wondered whether I had joined the ranks of those who publicly go over the edge and end up as fodder on some amused observer's bulletin board.

One remarkable thing about New York, especially among the gays, is how everyone seems to know each other, despite the fact that there are millions of people in the city. In the wake of our raid on Calvin's office, as we were making plans to disrupt an upcoming Council of Fashion Designers dinner at which Calvin was an awardee, I got a call from an acquaintance who wrote for *New York* magazine.

"Dan, my God!" he exclaimed. "Why didn't you just *meet* with Calvin?"

"We had a better chance of meeting with Elvis," I deadpanned. "We tried and tried, with him and with everyone else, and never heard back. We're inconvenient, I'm afraid."

"Well, I know him pretty well, and I bet he'd meet, if you promise to leave your paint at home."

"Thanks, just say when and I'm there, but don't get your hopes up."

A few days later, back at PETA's headquarters in Washington, I answered a call from a very pleasant-sounding woman from New York who said her name was Lynn Tesoro; she was Calvin's head of public relations, calling to set up a meeting. As she cordially continued, I jumped up from my desk and waved my free hand to quietly get everyone's attention, then dramatically pointed at the phone and silently mouthed the words *"Calvin's office."* Nobody had the slightest idea what I was trying to say, they just looked at me like I was having a Tourette's outburst.

"Can you be back in New York next Tuesday morning?" Lynn asked.

"Yes, of course," I said. "And don't worry—I'll bring flowers this time instead of paint." I even wore a suit.

Ironically, I was much more nervous going into Calvin's office as an invited guest rather than as an intruder. There was so much at stake, and there were so many eyes upon us. A columnist from the *Daily News* had called for an update on the campaign; I told her that Calvin had agreed to discuss the issue in person, and she wrote about it on the morning of our meeting. I figured that the more people knew about it, the more pressure he'd be under to respond sensibly. It was the first thing Calvin brought up.

"Good to meet you, Dan," Calvin said cautiously, in his rich Long Island lilt, as Lynn and I entered his spacious office. "But why did you tell the press about this meeting?"

"Well, first, they asked, and second, nobody said not to," I replied as we shook hands. He smirked and motioned for me to have a seat on the sofa as he sat in a chair facing me over a cluttered coffee table. I was a bit defensive after his first question, but quickly decided that it was probably good for him to sense some continued recklessness on our part. I tried to appear calm and collected, but inside I was an anxious jumble, trying to discern the best way to steer the meeting based on Calvin's reactions. Was I here just so that he could say he met with PETA and then continue to ignore our concerns? Might he actually be considering dumping fur, and if so, what would the tipping point be?

Like all designers, Klein socializes with celebrities, especially those who frequent the Hamptons, so I tried the name-dropping route. "Alec Baldwin and Kim Basinger are both PETA supporters," I said, "and they'll be thrilled when you renounce fur." He raised an eyebrow and lightly nodded, but he wasn't reaching for the peace pipe. Maybe it was better to try more intimidation.

"Also, you should know that we have plans to disrupt the Council of Fashion Designers dinner," I said like an unabashed whippersnapper, "but we would love nothing more than to call the whole thing off."

"Dan." Calvin sighed. "Let's just talk this through without threats, okay?"

"Oh, all right," I said, looking down sheepishly and moving on to a simpler, more straightforward, personal approach.

"You know, I bet under different circumstances we'd be friends. I can tell that you are a decent guy. But we can't let the fashion industry sweep these animal issues under the carpet. If you would simply allow yourself to see the cruelty you are personally responsible for when you use fur, you would change your mind. This is the easiest decision you'll ever make."

I pulled a video from my black canvas briefcase.

"My words mean very little," I continued. "These images mean a lot. This is a copy of the tape we sent—you really need to watch it and then make up your mind."

"I didn't receive any video," he said, a bit irritated. "But leave it, and I'll watch it."

I scanned the office, and, against the far wall, saw a large television.

"The tape is only four minutes long—we'll watch it now." I crossed the room, put the tape in the VCR, and started pressing buttons.

"I don't really have time just now," Calvin said as I fumbled with the machine.

"I'm not going anywhere until you watch the tape," I declared with a scathing smile, relieved to sense the agenda item on which to stake the meeting.

"Fine," he said, throwing his hands up with an exasperated laugh. Calvin called an assistant in to get the TV going, while I steadfastly waited next to it with my arms folded.

Finally the screen flickered on, followed by the images of docile chinchillas being genitally electrocuted, struggling beavers being drowned, minks having their necks crudely snapped, frenzied coyotes trying to gnaw their leg off to escape traps, and baby seals being clubbed to death in front of their shrieking mothers. Calvin watched, at first a bit awkwardly and dutifully, but soon the horror on his face showed that he wasn't heartless. He turned away only when the animals' piercing screams made the tape a bit too much to bear. To go a little easier on my host, I turned the volume down.

There were several seconds of continued silence after it ended.

"Well, that's it," he huffed, his moist eyes looking away pensively. "I have avoided looking at that crap for years."

"And . . . ?" I prodded, carefully.

"And that's it. I'm out. No more fur."

I wanted to feel ecstatic, but there were uncomfortable details to tend to. I pulled out the latest copy of *Fur World* and opened it to the page that listed Calvin among the designers who'd just signed a deal to produce a fur collection the next fall.

"What about this?" I asked.

He took it from my hands and looked at the article closely, then plopped it on the table.

"Let's just say you can't believe everything you read," he replied. "Different companies license my name for different fashion lines, and sometimes it's hard to keep track of what everyone is doing, but that fur line won't happen, and that's that."

"Terrific," I said. "But I need it in writing."

"Lynn!" he called out. "Would you please draft a statement we can release with PETA? We're out of the fur business." The incredible scene slowly started to feel real, but I fought any outward jubilation and tried to remain businesslike as Calvin walked me out.

The following Friday, a headline in the *New York Times*

stated, CALVIN KLEIN SAYS HE'LL NO LONGER PRODUCE FURS. The lengthy article, which detailed PETA's blitzkrieg attack and subsequent meeting, including the screening of the grisly videotape, began:

Calvin Klein ruffled the $1.1 billion fur industry yesterday, announcing that he would no longer produce furs. Citing "my own reflections on the humane treatment of animals" and "the fact that the fur segment of our business did not fit with our corporate policy any longer," Mr. Klein ended 17 years of licensing agreements.

The week following Calvin's landmark announcement coincided with Mardi Gras, which I had plans to celebrate with my happy-go-lucky alcoholic friend Brad, who lived in New Orleans. Brad greeted me at Louis Armstrong Airport with a big congratulatory hug and little bags of my three favorite flavors of Zapp's potato chips: Cajun Dill, Mesquite BBQ, and Hoppin' Jalapeño.

"We're gonna paint the town red as Calvin's office!" Brad yelped in his Texas twang.

With his warm round eyes and Lone Star tattoo, Brad was an exuberant, generous character that everybody wanted to be around, the perfect diversion from my usual responsibility-strewn warpath. He was one of the Bible Belt revelers I got to know while promoting the "Don't Kill the Animals" song in nightclubs.

Brad grew up in a crowded cabin on a dairy farm in a rural East Texas town with a road sign that once declared: WELCOME TO QUITMAN, WHERE THE SOIL IS BLACK AND THE

PEOPLE ARE WHITE. Whenever the truck came to haul away the baby calves so that their mothers could be drained of milk before being artificially inseminated again, Brad would ask his mother, Melba, why the cows wailed so sadly for three days.

"Close your ears, we're not supposed to think about that part," she replied in her weary drawl.

Brad explained to me how the dairy trade and the veal trade work hand in hand; the female calves are brought up to be milk machines like their mothers, but the male calves are sent off to be confined in veal crates where they can't move, so that their meat stays tender. These sickly calves, prematurely separated from their mothers, desperately suck on anything, a trait that some of the cruder farmhands took advantage of when they were horny, Brad recalled with disgust. Whenever anyone asked why I stick to soy milk and soy cheese, Brad piped up with these firsthand observances. The stories invariably met with silence, followed by a hastily changed subject.

One cold, dark Christmas, Brad gave in to my years of begging and brought me from New Orleans to Quitman. His volatile father had long since died, but we were warmly welcomed by Melba at a rural honky-tonk, where she was drinking Crown Royal with her jovial, crusty, one-eyed boyfriend, Doyle.

"What happened to your eye?" Brad asked.

"*Woodpecker got it!*" Doyle barked, bulging out his remaining eye and letting out a deep chuckle.

Near us on a barstool was a skinny bleached-blond middle-aged deaf woman with camel toe–tight jeans, who was so thrilled to see a new face that she threw a quarter in the jukebox and pulled me to my feet.

"Dance wit me!" she grunted with a wide smile and a severely impeded voice. "Ah cain't hear da music but ah can feel da beat!"

The classic rock tune, "What's Your Name?" blared out of the speakers. To be polite, I danced with her, though I think she based her moves more on the rhythm of the blinking holiday lights than the music. When the song ended, she wouldn't let me sit down. Then she began feeling me up, in front of God and everyone.

"I'm sorry!" I shouted, as if she could hear me better, my voice ricocheting around the bar.

"I'M GAY!"

The next thing I knew, I was in the dark parking lot, where Brad had dragged me with whiplash speed.

"Dan, its bad enough I was born here, I don't want to die here."

Brad had left Quitman in the early 1980s on the day he graduated from high school, a cute small-town boy who hit the big city and went crazy. A bit too crazy. Brad became one of AIDS' first customers, back before there were drugs to offset the disease. But he tried not to let his early death sentence get him down; he just figured he would party harder and go out with a smile on his face. Fortunately, Brad expired before New Orleans did; seeing his favorite city perish would have sent him off with a grimace. In any case, he died with his eyes wide open, not wanting to miss a thing right up to the bitter end.

Perhaps because of wonderful Brad's limited time on earth, I regularly exceeded the limit on my credit card to visit him and his easygoing little sister, Dawn, in their adopted Crescent City, staying in their progressively ramshackle apartments: the quaint one on St. Ann, the shotgun shack on Bourbon Street, and finally the dilapidated hovel with broken windows in the Marignie district, where we shopped with food stamps.

On the trip following the Calvin affair, we spent much of the time sipping bourbon and ginger ale at Lafitte's Blacksmith Shop, the famous archaic hot spot that looks like it should have collapsed long ago. I was fairly hung over when I spilled off Brad's couch to catch my flight back to Washington. Only I didn't return to Washington. I awoke to an urgent message from the office to fly instead to New York, to deal with the avalanche of interest in our new fashion campaign.

In PETA's formative years, I would do a lot and talk about it a little, but as the organization and our impact grew, I found myself doing a bit less and talking about it nonstop due to increased media interest. This was gratifying in one way, but also frustrating, so I endeavored to make each interview action-oriented in order to be more productive. When *New York* magazine devoted its Fashion Week issue to PETA—a cover story called "Radical Chic"—I had the writer accompany me to department-store fur salons, where I quizzed salespeople on the death methods used on each type of coat; they rarely knew, but always called security.

When a reporter from the *New Yorker* invited me to lunch at Zen Palate to dissect the Calvin raid, I had her shadow me afterward to Fifth Avenue, where I inconspicuously plastered mink-clad shoppers with stickers that read, I'M AN ASSHOLE—I WEAR FUR. (Write, and I'll send you some.) I carry these handy stickers in my nonleather wallet every winter, and people never know what hit 'em—not necessarily because I'm sly, but because fur pads you like a walrus. I once stickered Joan Rivers and Cindy Adams at a premiere, though I felt bad later and wrote them a note; I don't really think they are assholes, I think they are hilarious, I just wish they'd consider the plight of animals other than their pampered purebred dogs. I must give Cindy credit, however—she was bold enough to print my note in her column in the *New York Post*.

Increasingly, my New York nights were becoming as productive as the busy days. I not only crashed at Goldy's loft, I also tagged along with him to endless rounds of parties, and he introduced me to many helpful friends. Among them were fashion photographer Steven Klein, who helped get Christy Turlington to pose for our first RATHER GO NAKED THAN WEAR FUR poster, and no-nonsense nightclub impresario Steve Lewis, who officially banned fur from his thriving clubs, including Tunnel, Life, Spa, and Home. At each venue, Steve installed a plaque at the door that read THE ONLY WILDLIFE HERE IS HUMAN: NO FUR COATS ALLOWED. He has refused entry to Jennifer Lopez, P. Diddy, Axl Rose, and much of the editorial staff of Italian *Vogue*, which had rented one of his clubs for a private party. They were forced to use a limo around the block as their coat room.

More and more designers started speaking up for PETA, most notably Todd Oldham, who did a line of PETA fake-fur hats; Marc Bouwer, who partnered with us for a cruelty-free fashion show, and later Stella McCartney, who got the Gucci Group to back her high-end nonleather shoe line. Surprisingly, given our hardcore approach, I was even asked to model a few designers' duds: Issey Miyake's Manhattan office had some of his animal-free clothes shipped over from Tokyo for me to wear in a PETA spread he sponsored in the Japanese fashion magazine *Dansen*, and the kindhearted Cuban designer Manolo stitched me a taupe linen suit to show off at his packed Central Park West runway show.

Even the *New York Times* had me pose for the cover of their Sunday Style section—in a WWI combat outfit, complete with helmet, old-fashioned industrial paint gun, and a cuddly rabbit on my knee. This was the fall-back setup because the photographer couldn't get a permit for a tank to be rolled out onto Seventh Avenue. The article was titled ANTI-FUR CAMPAIGNER CHARMS HIS WAY TO THE HEIGHTS OF FASHION, which felt absurd, since I still resided at the bottom of a friend's messy closet.

One gratifying Friday night, things came full circle with Calvin Klein. We literally ran into each other at Wonderbar in the East Village, the vagabond neighborhood I love because it feels cut off from the boring business side of Manhattan. This was the "different circumstance" I had imagined when I told Calvin in his office that we might well be friends. We had a sociable exchange, swapped numbers, and over the next few months sampled each others' worlds; I brought him to the tranny punk dive Squeezebox, which he found more interesting than the bar at the Four Seasons, and he brought me to the elegant Italian restaurant Bottino, which I found more interesting than Burritoville. We chatted not just about animal rights and fashion but about our favorite escape destinations, how gays overstyle, and how to create a sensational ad campaign. Once his driver carted us around to a few clubs, where an endless parade of youngsters pulled their pants low to show Calvin his name on their underwear. He was always cordial, waiting until we had safely passed them by before he rolled his eyes. Considering that I had helped terrify much of his staff and had vandalized his office, Calvin was very good-natured when asked by a reporter about our unlikely association.

"I think more about Dan's concerns than his tactics," Calvin said. "I'm sympathetic, and we've become friends."

Of course, not all the designers were sympathetic, but at least, now, many agreed to meet, including Marc Jacobs. I showed Marc the same stomach-turning fur tape that I had showed Calvin.

"Plastic surgery isn't pretty to watch either, but look at the results," he said, matter-of-factly.

Marc's comparison of elective cosmetic surgery to animals being forcibly mutilated and killed was a stretch, but I listened, hoping to discern what makes an intelligent person think like this. I learned that the brain isn't always connected to the heart. I also learned that, like me, Marc is comfortable around those who hold opposing beliefs. Oddly, we had an easy rapport and found that we shared a similar sense of humor and taste in music, so we made plans to see one of our favorite bands, the Voluptuous Horror of Karen Black. We became friends, occasionally meeting for dinner or drinks, and he regularly introduced me to PETA-friendly stylists and photographers. Marc even invited me to his runway shows— those without fur, of course. But the friendship understandably fizzled when we started disrupting fashion shows, including his. I did leave him a courteous message about it.

Other designers were less interesting, and less sincere. Portly Oscar de la Renta had me meet him in his office, where he shook my hand and told me he wouldn't renew his fur license—then a few months later went right back on his word. It was as if my meeting had merely been with a bulging, bald mannequin. John Galliano invited me to his stately abode in Paris, where we had a very urbane chat in a dimly lit room. He explained, with those ever-bleary eyes and raspy voice, that he wasn't really a "fur person," but that

Bernard Arnault, the money man behind his luxury company, insisted he use real fur to keep prices high. John's next collection included an outfit featuring not just fur but a cap made of the entire face of a skinned silver fox, the animal's lifeless eyes sloping down just above the model's lifeless eyes. Priceless.

Most crass of all was Michael Kors, who told me, hands aflutter, "If people will buy it, I'll design *anything*." This includes karakul—street name broadtail lamb—which is made from the skins of baby sheep who are killed either by a painful induced miscarriage or by being bludgeoned to death just after they are born. Their wool must remain baby soft. Unlike kittens, these lambs open their eyes at birth, just in time to see a violent man hammer them with a club several times. That is their entire experience on this planet.

How could any human being defend this atrocious cruelty, especially when the "fabric" is so easily mimicked synthetically, without any blood and guts?

"It's really *drapey*," was Michael Kors's justification. So much for the notion that all homosexuals are more sophisticated and sensitive.

Why are certain designers and fashion editors so obsessed with fur, year after year? Of course, some people will do anything for money, but another theory is Cruella De Vil syndrome. Let me explain. Furry animals are naturally beautiful. Fur's biggest proponents are, to be polite, not natural beauties. For those unfamiliar with the key players, Michael Kors has a bulbous red face and receding wiry hair, which he inexplicably bleaches. *Vogue* editor Anna Wintour, who not only bullies young fur-free designers and models but ran a story on why potatoes are tastier when fried in horse lard, looks as if she has constant, painful gas. This may explain why equally pretentious and vulgar fur lover Karl Lagerfeld always carries that fan. And Donatella Versace? Well, I rest my case. Since the whole point of fashion is to decorate yourself in the hopes of improving your appearance, perhaps, like Cruella, the fur-obsessed try to compensate for their unfortunate looks by stealing the beauty of another.

These are the individuals for whom the expression "all style and no substance" was invented. I had these parasites in mind when I was asked by *Genre* magazine, which had included me on its list of influential gays, who *I* thought was a notable homosexual.

"Andrew Cunanan," I replied, almost instinctively, "because he got Gianni Versace to stop using fur."

The day the issue hit newsstands, I learned that serial killer humor is one of the few remaining taboos. Headlines trumpeted the "sick pointed joke," Naomi Campbell issued a statement that she was "aghast," and a national news crew ambushed me as I sleepily walked off a plane. I instantly phoned the magazine to tell them they were free to disown me.

Astonishingly, *Genre*'s savvy editor in chief, Morris Wiesinger, defended me on television, saying that the quip was merely an example of the provocative campaigning that led them to put me on their list in the first place. The publisher went even further and offered me a monthly column. The yearlong series, titled "Out on the Road," gave me the opportunity to file Mark Twainish dispatches from some of the odd places I ended up and about some of the peculiar characters I encountered.

So began my moonlighting career as a writer. Joking about killing? It's a living.

Father knows best.

CHAPTER 9

An Alpine Diversion

Zurich's Café Odeon is a bustling Art Nouveau hangout around the corner from where the narrow Limmat River flows into glorious Lake Zurich, in the shadow of the Alps. It hasn't changed much since it opened in 1911. The curved wooden bar with brass coat hooks underneath is surrounded by tightly arranged rows of polished marble tables around which the efficient servers twist and bend while holding aloft trays of drinks that never seem to spill. Like most structures in Switzerland, there's a lot going on within a very small space. Lenin, Trotsky, and Mussolini drank within these ornate walls, as did Mata Hari, the stripper who made exotic dancing socially acceptable in Paris before she was put on trial for espionage during World War I. "Harlot, yes, but traitor, never," she said before being riddled with bullets by the firing squad. During World War II, all sorts of spies met in neutral Switzerland at the famed Odeon to exchange information. Loving a theme, this is where I arranged my Sunday-morning rendezvous with the prolific undercover agent behind many of PETA's intercontinental exposés.

By now, I had been promoted to director of international campaigns for the organization. This newly developed position involved trotting the globe as a crafty infiltrator, a job not unlike 007's—if 007 wore silly costumes instead of snazzy tuxedos, that is.

For example, when world leaders convened in Rio de Janeiro for the environmental Earth Summit, they locked out any discussion of the meat trade's central role in deforestation, drought, and the contamination of rivers and bays. To draw attention to this, my friend Julia and I—she dressed as a cow and I as a blood-spattered butcher—burst into the Summit's dining area, where I "slaughtered" her with a giant steel meat cleaver bearing the message "Earth Summit Solution: Vegetarianism." The officials upon whose table we leaped weren't pleased, but the previously bored reporters were; they interviewed us at length about the issue, even having us repeat the message on TV in their various languages. The image even made the front page of the *Washington Post* Style section the next morning. Smuggling the simple costumes inside was easy, and to get the massive metal blade past the Summit's rifle-toting soldiers, we merely wrapped it in cardboard, plastered it with DELEGATE stickers snagged from an official reception, and said it was a pie chart.

A more subtle masquerade worked at Gillette's world headquarters in Boston. In order to breach security there, my colleague Peter and I dressed as janitors and wheeled a large television right past the guard desk, into an elevator, and up to the cafeteria. We plugged it in by the cash register in front of a line of dismayed executives and held an impromptu screening of PETA's fresh undercover tape showing how the company blinded and poisoned rabbits and rats to test everything from shaving cream to Liquid Paper. We ended up in jail, but Gillette soon stopped using animals.

Sitting and waiting at the little table at Café Odeon, I sipped my second coffee and pondered the most recent caper.

I had arrived in Zurich, the distinguished capital of banking, from Milan, the hedonistic capital of fashion. There, dressed as a Catholic priest, I had gained entry into fur designer Gianfranco Ferré's packed runway show.

With my rusty Italian, a serene smile, and wearing pretend reading glasses, I explained at both check-in desks that I wasn't on a list, but that "Mr. Ferré is a patron of our parish and invited me at the last minute for good luck." It worked. I limped in among the 800 air-kissing guests with a banner rolled up in my rigid black pant leg that read, THOU SHALT NOT KILL, alongside an antifur logo. When the show started, I calmly unfurled the sign and overtook the catwalk in a blizzard of flashbulbs, sending a pro-animal message around the world via the paparazzi jammed by the dozens on a three-tiered platform. Ad campaigns are prohibitively expensive for a charity, especially one targeting so many powerful industries; hijacking an adversary's media event to reach the public usually only costs a few bruised limbs—and a few bruised egos.

The confused models clogged up behind me, and the blaring music stopped cold, replaced by the clamor of buyers and editors scampering from their seats for a better look at what was causing the ruckus. I didn't chant any slogans or scream any epithets, but rather kept in clergylike character and gave a stern Father Knows Best scowl at the gathering throngs like they were pitiable sinners for promoting the ungodly fur trade. *If only they knew I had originally bought this getup for Halloween.* The perplexed security men tried to snatch my banner and prod me off the runway, but I wouldn't budge. They huddled, eyeing me like I was a mad gorilla who had escaped from the zoo, then finally charged and tackled me onto my back. Shocked at this use of force against a "man of the cloth," a small group of distraught Italian ladies sprang from the first row, clutching the crosses on their dainty necklaces, and swatted the guards with their programs, screaming "Leave the priest alone!"

The most difficult part of the endeavor was containing my laughter at this point. With a different guard yanking each limb, I was dragged down three flights of stairs and tossed onto the dusty street, where the kind carabinieri who had been summoned refused to arrest me. In fact, they protected me when Ferré's furious organizer yelled that I had ruined the show and tried to punch me. "My son," I said to the livid fashionista, even though he was older than me, "how would you have explained to your mother that you hit a priest with glasses?" With a more authentic limp and an even more serene smile, I disappeared into the subway, went back to my hotel, and packed for Zurich.

It was as toasty inside the Odeon as it was frosty outside, which made the café's grand windows steam up and obscure the well-dressed passersby heading around the corner and uphill to the cathedral. I woke up in my room on that cold Sunday morning to the pealing of Zurich's Gothic church bells. After channel-surfing between solemn religious services and grainy reruns of *CHiPs* and *Charlie's Angels*, dubbed in German, I bundled up in my flannel-lined jeans and black rubber jacket and went for a stroll through the city's drizzly storybook streets before my meeting with the investigator Mark Rissi. I can use his real name because he is already known in European media circles and uses a variety of aliases when conducting investigations. I had spent the previous day in Mark's claustrophobic editing suite, screening hours of the latest unsettling footage he'd obtained in his travels. Today, we had to strategize how to turn these undercover cases into public campaigns.

"You always make me meet you here, where parking is impossible," Mark said with a grin as he approached my table at the Odeon and took off his coat. "Couldn't we get together where you are staying?"

"The room I rented is directly above a fondue restaurant, and the minute they start boiling the cheese, the whole place smells like dirty socks," I said with a nauseated look. "Fortunately, my airplane earplugs fit up my nose."

Mark has thick graying brown hair and a neatly trimmed beard and mustache that perfectly fit his academic demeanor. He lives with his girlfriend in the hills just outside of Zurich. His background is producing films for Swiss television, and in 1974 he did a caustic short called *The Coat*, in which a woman decides to abandon her fur in the coat room after her rugged dinner date shares his experiences on the Canadian traplines, complete with graphic flashbacks. The issue of animals being killed for fashion was almost unheard of at the time, and the fur trade wanted to keep it that way. They filed a lawsuit that delayed the film's broadcast by a year—prompting Mark to probe even more deeply into the skittish industry. They claimed that most fur coats came not from trapped animals but from those farm-raised in northern Europe, especially Finland. Mark instantly booked a ticket to Helsinki. With the help of a lovely blond biologist who acted as his cover and translator, he documented how foxes and minks, who roam miles in the wild each day, go nuts in their cages on fur farms and pace neurotically before being slaughtered just as their first winter coat thickens. The biologist also pointed out that, like dogs and cats, these animals have a very powerful sense of smell and would never eat or sleep where they crap, and thus confinement to these tiny, reeking wire boxes causes many of the frustrated animals to mutilate themselves.

It was the world's first peek at the ugly underbelly of the global industry that had for more than a century simply passed off fur coats as the ultimate status symbol. With no sensible defense, the Finnish fur trade attempted a smear campaign, charging that Mark and his lady accomplice must have been taking money from the companies that produce fake fur in an underhanded ruse to cut into their sales. They couldn't seem to fathom that one could be motivated by human decency, or even journalistic curiosity. Mark shared his findings with animal protection groups, and after his more sweeping exposés aired, fur sales fell by 70 percent in Switzerland and were also impacted elsewhere in Europe. Within a few years fur farms had closed throughout much of Finland, where the sweet young biologist was publicly branded a traitor and spat upon in the street.

I first heard about Mark in the mid-1980s, when I began coordinating PETA's antifur campaign. I had accepted an invitation to tour what the fur industry touted as the world's most modern, humane fox farm, in Holland, back before that country outlawed all fox farms. The wary foxes eyed our little group, fearfully scurrying to the backs of their cages at the slightest move, even if it was just somebody checking his watch. I can only imagine their panic later, away from our view, when one by one they were wrenched, yelping, with a catchpole and had metal rods forced between their teeth and into their rectums, their paws jutting out violently as the electric current passed through their bodies. Among our skeptical bunch was a Dutch animal rights leader who told me that if I was to be an expert on the issue, I must meet with Mark Rissi, the Swiss filmmaker who routinely gained access to seedy facilities around the world that use all kinds of animals for all kinds of things.

On my first visit to Zurich, I found Mark in his small studio at Swiss television. After he showed me his just-finished exposé on the live dog meat markets in Seoul, he told me that while he was there he had been able to trespass onto a massive new fur farm setup in rural South Korea primarily for export to America. The company was called Jindo.

"I know it well," I said. "They have forty stores across the States, and the CEO brags that they intend to mass-market mink and become 'the McDonald's of fur.'"

"Well, take a look at this," Mark said, putting an unedited tape into the machine. "And excuse the background noise; this place is very close to the North Korean border, and U.S. Army helicopters were constantly flying overhead." Mark had learned that the remote fur farm had been built with Danish advisers using Danish-bred minks. Noting that no telephone wires seemed to connect this rustic outpost to the outside world—especially the company's main office—Mark told the workers that he was a Danish videographer sent by Jindo headquarters in Seoul to document the bustling farm's progress. The manager happily gave him a tour. It was summertime, very hot and humid, and the minks, who are naturally water dwellers, languished in their cages and panted heavily, barely able to lift their heads. The manager answered all of Mark's questions, including the one about death methods.

"Well, you know—" He started to giggle. "We kill the animals using the same system as Germans used to kill the Jewish people in World War II," he said proudly on camera. "We gas them."

He then courteously directed Mark to the nearby fox farm, where workers demonstrated how they kill the mostly female foxes by swinging them by the tail between two wooden boards hinged at the bottom; when the fox is caught in the planks, a rope is cinched over the top of the boards to slowly crush the life out of her. "It costs nothing and does not harm the fur," said a farmhand on the video.

With a rough edit of this tape, I left Zurich a much-keyed-up twenty-four-year-old. Back at the PETA headquarters in Washington, Ingrid and I pondered who among our supporters had a suitably authoritative voice to narrate the Jindo video and spearhead the campaign. The choice was simple: Bea Arthur, then in her *Golden Girls* heyday. Next stop, Hollywood, where Bea, wearing a loose white turtleneck and a long vest, filmed the introduction to our new exposé right on the show's living room set after an exhaustive Friday-night taping. Both Rue McClanahan and Betty White stayed to watch, and afterward joined Bea on the set's couch to film a PETA antifur commercial. The show's kind director and the whole *Golden Girls* crew stayed late, free of charge, so that I was able to walk away with a slickly produced tape. Within a few weeks, the video was airing on news stations across the country in conjunction with PETA protests at Jindo stores. As usual, the furriers proclaimed that our protests merely attracted more customers, but in reality business quickly dried up. Within months the company abandoned its plans to mass-market fur coats in America, and every single one of Jindo's dozens of stores closed.

Since then, every year or so, I go to Zurich, one of the world's most picturesque cities, to pore over some of the world's most grotesque images, with an eye to adapting them into consumer education campaigns. On this trip, the day before our meeting at the Odeon, I sat in Mark's dark little studio and watched shrieking geese pinned between the knees of hefty Hungarian women who were plucking them bald and bloody for fluffy down pillows and comforters; struggling ducks being force-fed with hydraulic pumps in France to fatten their livers to make pâté de foie gras; and flailing turtles on a dock in the South Seas, where they had been turned upside down and, fully conscious, were having the meat carved out of them for export in pricey soup, their flipperlike limbs waving helplessly.

It's not the sort of stuff that makes you want to twirl around the Alps like Julie Andrews in *The Sound of Music*. In fact, it can get downright depressing. To keep from getting too morose, I try to build in little breaks. My favorite Swiss diversion is going window-shopping for cuckoo clocks. I've never bought one, but I love looking. There are so many different kinds, with so many different figurines that pop out and twirl around to the enchanting music: beer-stein-brandishing barmen, blond pigtailed Heidi lookalikes, and little wooden mountain climbers with painted-on lederhosen. It would be impossible to pick a favorite, so I just push each clock's big hand ahead to the next hour in order to enjoy the chime for a little while in the cheery shop before getting back to ugly reality in the studio.

In one sense Mark and I have similar jobs, in that we both assume various guises to infiltrate the industries that use animals. Of course, the big difference is that I usually just confront the gluttonous, aloof professionals in their ivory towers, whereas he goes to the gut-wrenching ground floor and gets his hands dirty. Sometimes, very dirty. It's a good thing that the Café Odeon has a constant din of conversations in several languages and loud jazz music wafting through the air, because our discussions tend to be a bit unappetizing.

Mark told me about a trip in which he stowed away in a filthy truck bringing cattle from Poland to Spain to document the standard transport cruelties such as broken bones, severe dehydration, and chronic diarrhea. In Europe this issue is known as "live export," and in the United States as "downed cow," because after their odyssey some of the animals are too weak to even make it up the ramp to slaughter and instead tumble pathetically to the ground. As Mark was covertly filming inside the shit-filled truck near a hillside village in the Pyrenees, he was discovered and ejected and had to hitch a ride to an airport for a hasty flight home.

"The stewardesses isolated me in business class because of the putrid stench," Mark laughed. "It was very embarrassing—they wanted to dump a bottle of duty-free cologne over me."

My favorite of his adventures occurred in the early 1990s, when much of the world was busy celebrating the collapse of communism in a disarrayed Soviet Union. Mark used the opportunity to smuggle in suitcases carrying enough bottles of veterinary narcotics to peacefully put to sleep every creature from Kiev to St. Petersburg. He had been summoned by desperate animal advocates in Moscow, where starving, sickly dogs not only roamed the streets but were captured by loutish dog catchers who were paid per pooch. Among the top clients were the laboratory at the University of Moscow and the Budka slaughterhouse in Pirogovo, which made a killing exporting dog skin as designer watchband leather. Mark filmed one tearful old woman imploring these city workers to let her dog go, but they laughed in her face and drove off.

As the Soviet government dissolved and people toasted its demise amid bonfires, Mark and some local animal people went underground into the university's all-but-abandoned laboratory, in a black-and-white-tiled cellar, lit only by a single dangling bulb. When they pried open the door, the rancid smell was unimaginable. There they found dozens of semiconscious dogs shivering in piles of their own feces with untreated open wounds from derelict heart and bone experiments. With a carefully administered needle and a gentle pat on the head, Mark and his posse put these poor mutts out of their misery.

Oddly enough, it was at this gloomy scene that Mark met some unlikely heroes: a pair of shocked science students who not only helped in the mission of mercy in the de-bolted basement, but agreed to help him uncover another mysterious facility they had heard about. It was in the nearby town of Pushkino, and it looked like a Siberian prison camp, complete with a high brick wall covered in barbed wire and two watchtowers. It was Russia's largest fur farm, when that country supplied a third of the world's fur. Goaded by the suffering they found in the secret basement, the young Soviets eagerly agreed to help Mark intrude in order to film whatever was going on inside. True to their word, the duo picked Mark up early the next morning in a battered, rusty truck, and even brought him some genuine Russian workman's coveralls and glasses. Making their way to Pushkino, one of his new comrades suggested that they pose as a detachment of scientists with an official order from the Ministry of Agriculture to inspect the farm. Since Mark didn't speak any Russian, they decided to pass him off as a mute scientist who specialized in animal feed.

They approached the menacing gates and bravely announced themselves as inspectors. The manager was called, and he nervously rushed in, hastily inviting the visi-

tors to the canteen, where it was clear that he aimed to lubri-
cate the "inspectors" with enough vodka to keep them from
noticing anything amiss at the facility. They exchanged dirty
jokes and chortled heartily, and as Mark was "mute" but not
"deaf," he had to act as if he understood, following along and
laughing at just the right moments. The manager stalled as
long as he could, but the crafty new spies finally insisted on
a tour. As in the fetid laboratory basement, the stench was
enough to knock out a heavyweight. Mark lagged a bit
behind the group, aiming his small video camera at row after
filth-encrusted row of cages crammed not just with squirming minks and foxes but the famous black sables as well as an
incredibly docile animal that he knew well from the Alps but
never expected to see screaming and thrashing about in a
moldy cage: marmots, who in nature hibernate underground.

Once safely back outside the compound, the courageous
young Russians were so jubilant that their stunt had
remained undetected that they made a special detour to show
Mark the KGB headquarters, notorious for its labyrinth of
underground prison cells. They knew well that had they been
caught, they might well have ended up there. The footage
soon hit airwaves across Europe and further soured the public's opinion about fur. Hearing these stories of human
courage helps blunt the impact of the atrocious cruelty at the
center of our conversations at the Odeon.

"Are we eating?" asked Mark.

"After the videos you showed me yesterday, I'm not so
hungry," I replied. "And I'm not much of a breakfast person
anyway."

"I'll get a basket of fruit and rolls we can pick at," he
said, flagging down a busy waiter.

Mark had just returned from China, which had recently

overtaken the United States, Europe, and Russia as the world's largest fur supplier. With cheap labor and no laws protecting animals, China is the favorite production hub for American and European fashion companies. The day before, Mark had showed me brand-new tapes from a massive investigation he coordinated with Chinese animal advocates who were just as brave as the Russians he had worked with. They secretly filmed on fur farms in China's southern Hebei Province, where animals are literally nailed to a board and skinned alive, the only hairs left on their heaving, white pulpous bodies being their pitifully fluttering eyelashes.

I'm not an emotional type who gets easily distressed by horrible images—as long as I am able to do something, anything, to help stop it. The only times I get down are when I learn about some atrocity, think about it, and realize that, for reasons of priorities, practicalities, or lack of staffing or budget, there's nothing we can do to change it, at least for the time being. Toward the end of my visits to Zurich, after having screened hours of devastating footage and figuring out what we can turn into a campaign and what we can't, I tend to get a bit depressed. That's another reason why I frequent the Odeon to map things out—the atmosphere is so festive that it's hard to feel too low.

On this Sunday morning, it didn't take more than an hour for Mark and me to make our battle plans. Instead of pushing for Chinese legislation that would likely never be enforced, we would use Mark's tapes to target designers and companies that use Chinese fur and push for them to drop fur altogether (among the big names we convinced were J. Crew and Ralph Lauren). And we reckoned we could use the French footage of the force-feeding of the ducks to bolster a proposed law banning the production and sale of pâté de foie gras in California, one of the two U.S. states where it is produced (Governor Schwarzenegger eventually signed the landmark bill).

By the time Mark left, morning had given way to midday, and I had graduated from black coffee to red wine. The Odeon was getting packed, and much of the crowd now stood as they drank and chatted, since there was no place to sit. I was finalizing my notes and staring into space, trying to conceive of a way to use the awful footage of the geese being ravaged for their down, and of the helpless turtles being eviscerated for soup. Ever mindful not to spread PETA's limited resources too thin, I decided to shove these images to the back of my mind with the hope that someday an opportunity might arise in which we could bring them to consumers.

I must have had a somewhat forlorn look on my face when I caught the friendly gaze of an Italian mingling with his friends. He was thirtysomething with dark floppy hair and a wide smile. I smiled back, glad to be lifted out of my pensive doldrums for a second. Before long, he ambled over and introduced himself in very broken English. When I replied in Italian, he laughed, introduced himself as Massimo, sat down where Mark had been, and continued the conversation even more confidently in his native tongue.

"My two friends and I drove to Zurich for the weekend from Lake Como, near Milan," he said, motioning the waiter to bring more wine. "We just checked out of the hotel and stopped here before heading back. It's such a fantastic drive, even though it can take six hours."

"I came up from Milan myself," I replied. "I was there for work last week and came here for work this weekend. I take the train back overnight and fly back to the States from Milan tomorrow."

"You work too much," he said. "How could you come all

the way to Switzerland and not see the Alps?" After a few minutes his friends came over and joined the conversation. Like most Italians, they were a very warm bunch. Before long, Massimo had a plan.

"We are only three in my car—why don't you drive with us back to Italy?" he offered. "You can stay with me near the lake in Como, and I'll drive you to the airport in Milan tomorrow. We're taking the Alpine road through Zug and Altdorf, and it's beautiful. You won't see the sights from a train window at night."

"Are you sure you have room at your place?" I asked

"It's not like he has a villa," one of his friends said, rolling his eyes, "but there's plenty of room."

I thought of the strict guidance that mothers give their children: *Never accept a ride from a stranger.* Then I remembered that my mother had never given me that tedious Puritanical warning.

"I'd love to come along!"

I quickly stuffed all my dreary notes into a folder and ran through the cobblestone streets like Charlie Bucket when he found the golden ticket in the Wonka bar. I checked out of my cheesy hotel and was back with my new Italian friends at the Odeon within half an hour. We whizzed out of Zurich with the radio blaring.

I dodged detailed questions about my job, as I didn't want to get stuck answering questions about animal rights for the rest of the day—it was time to clock out. And there are so many more interesting things to talk about when you're getting to know people, such as where they're from, favorite books and bands, and most embarrassing moments. As we entered the snowy foothills, I asked if there was an Alpine equivalent to the Donner party. They had never heard about that dramatic Rocky Mountain tale of cannibalism, so I explained it, perhaps a bit too enthusiastically; Massimo's friends exchanged slightly worried glances in the backseat as we wove our way into the misty mountains.

"Don't worry, guys, I'm a vegetarian!" I reassured them before changing the subject to the somewhat less gruesome topic of yodeling. Massimo wasn't fazed. In fact, he reached over and clasped my hand.

We didn't stop until we had driven above the cloud line. I learned that although much of Switzerland is bleak and foggy during the winter, the Alps are *so* massive that if you climb high enough, you can burst through the thick dark mist and be suddenly squinting from the sun. It was a fantastic sensation, like we were ascending into heaven, a feeling that I never thought I'd experience or even be eligible for. Massimo pulled over so that we could get out and enjoy the silence and the panoramic view. Tiny specks of the colossal mountains showed through the drifts of snow, making it look as if we were surrounded by towering mounds of chocolate chip ice cream. Below us there was no earth, just puffy clouds, and above a deep blue sky with a crescent moon rising. My new friend put his arm around me, and I kissed him on the cheek.

We arrived in the little village by Lake Como well after dark and dropped off Massimo's friends before heading to his house, which overlooked the lake. Despite his friend's assertion to the contrary, it indeed was a villa, a small, charming one, complete with a meandering stone path leading to a moonlit garden. Visiting places like this makes me thankful to have been raised in ugly postwar white trash apartments, because I have learned to appreciate every old brick in even mildly historic abodes. What's more, this villa had a washer and dryer, and I was able to discreetly cleanse my priest shirt of two messy Halloweens and one recent protest.

After finishing a load, Massimo and I drove down to the medieval town square in time to hit a late-night pizzeria. He must have thought that I was joking about being a vegetarian, because he continually offered me a bite of his ham-covered pizza. It did smell wonderful, but I wasn't really tempted.

"No, thanks," I said, thinking of poor Mata Hari's simple words: *Harlot, yes, but traitor, never.*

With Pam in our box overlooking the Vienna Opera Ball.

CHAPTER 10

Cinderfella

In 1913, as a penniless Adolph Hitler fled Vienna to dodge the draft, Emperor Franz Josef commissioned Richard Strauss to compose a special symphony for the grand opening of the city's Konzerthaus. Although opulent, with marble columns, wood-paneled boxes, red velvet seats, and ornate chandeliers dangling from a gold-trimmed ceiling, the hall is small enough to feel cozy. It survived two world wars and the rock and rap revolutions to remain a hot spot on Vienna's music scene.

Almost a century after it opened, near the end of Austria's formal winter ball season, the Konzerthaus played host to the candy trade's lavish Bon Bon Ball. At this annual dance, young ladies from different sectors of the industry vie for a sparkly tiara and the title of "Miss Bon Bon." When I walked in, I was struck by how exuberant the smartly dressed crowd was. Maybe everyone was on a sugar rush. Among the revelers were dancers costumed as oversize cookies, spice drops, and licorice twists, who spun around to give guests tasty samples of whichever confection they were impersonating. Aside from sweets, there wasn't a lot to eat, which meant the ever-flowing champagne went to work very quickly, easing my nerves about my impending assignment. The odd task had been hastily arranged when I was spotted on the red carpet by the party's portly host.

"*Meine Damen und Herren,* we have a surprise guest who takes the stage in ten minutes!" he announced just before midnight, his jovial German baritone echoing through the packed *haus.* "He is here to select Miss Bon Bon—Dan Mathews!"

Relieved to hear cheers instead of jeers, I calmly locked myself into the backstage bathroom to vomit champagne and marzipan before emerging to shake down the dancer dressed as a mint so that I had fresh breath for my celebratory waltz with the new candy queen, the poised Silvia Milde. She represented the chocolate makers.

No, this wasn't a bad dream induced by a tainted Toblerone, but the conclusion of an all-too-real trip to Europe's most conservative country, in which I unexpectedly went from reviled outlaw to guest of honor in less than a week. My gypsy life as an animal activist has led to some strange scenarios, but this Austrian odyssey takes the Sacher torte.

It can all be blamed on a blonde: Pamela Anderson. The story begins quite innocently.

Pamela was invited to the Vienna Opera Ball—the fanciest since balls became a Viennese pastime in the 1800s—by a publicity-savvy Austrian real estate mogul named Richard Lugner. In addition to attending the aristocratic affair, at which men wear white tie and tails and women wear showy gowns, the deal required her to sign autographs at Lugner City, one of Vienna's biggest shopping centers. As Pam had just posed for a new PETA poster, she opted to sign copies of that, and she invited me along to ensure that the cheesy mall gig would be promoted as a proper campaign launch. The poster's slogan, TURN OVER A NEW LEAF—TRY VEGETARIAN, ran across an image of Pamela wearing a skimpy bikini made of lettuce.

Work obligations aside, Pamela and I were so excited about the Cinderella-like Opera Ball that we began taking waltzing lessons, she with a private instructor at her home in Malibu, and me at the Fred Astaire School of Dance in a strip mall in Virginia Beach, near PETA's recently relocated headquarters. When the instructor asked why I was taking a crash course, I muttered that I'd been invited to a dance in Vienna; she nodded and said, "Oh, up near D.C.," and I didn't correct her. I had never waltzed before, but as I religiously watch *Lawrence Welk* reruns on PBS each Saturday night, I was vaguely familiar with the fancy footwork and learned quickly. Pam often refers to me as her gay husband, one who can escort her to the sort of cultural events that the rougher men in her life, like Tommy Lee and Kid Rock, might not appreciate. Neither of us imagined that my own bad reputation would soon transform our fairy-tale trip.

We were under the mistaken impression that our millionaire host, Richard Lugner, was formally connected with the ball; in fact, the actual organizers were upset that he was using the occasion of the high society event as a lowbrow publicity stunt for his shopping center, and it became a scandal in the local papers. To deflect criticism, Lugner quickly declared that Pamela's appearance would be not just to promote his mall but to launch an animal awareness campaign, and he disclosed that I would be her date. This defense backfired, however, when columnists did some online snooping and found that the man Herr Lugner was bringing to sit in his $15,000 box directly overlooking the festivities had been arrested for confronting opera-going fur wearers at La Scala and Lincoln Center, among other places.

An Austrian magazine ran an alarming protest photo in which I'm drenched in fake blood, looking much like Sissy Spacek in *Carrie*, with the headline GUESS WHO'S COMING TO THE OPERA BALL? The spread also featured a sultry shot of Pam—topless—and a photo of Lugner with his pretty trophy wife, Mausi, wrapped in a chinchilla coat. "Pam isn't the only one who strips," a Viennese furrier chortled in the story. "So does Mathews—I witnessed his nude protest at a fur convention in Hong Kong where he was duly arrested." The story ricocheted around Europe as society reporters wondered which dignitaries we intended to splash or flash. It was all very punk and exciting . . . if only it were true.

Lugner announced that he would station police officers in the box to restrain me, and mortified ball officials said they would make me sign a legal pledge not to throw paint on any furry fellow waltzers. Meanwhile, back in America, Pamela and I earnestly practiced our *one*-two-three moves to Mozart, completely oblivious to our supposed plot, until her agent received a call from Vienna's Grand Hotel, where Lugner had booked us.

"Guests are canceling reservations for fear Pamela's date attacks fur wearers in the lobby," said the nervous hotel manager. Then PETA's phones started ringing, first with Viennese lawyers asking for our fax number so I could sign papers swearing not to be a disruptive party pooper, then with reporters, many of whom desperately hoped we *were* planning something sneaky in order to spice up their coverage of the stuffy annual affair. I was blindsided by the calls and responded in a casual, lighthearted way.

"It must be a terrific place to protest fur," I explained, not wanting to discourage any groups considering targeting the event. "But Pamela and I are invited guests, so we'll use waltzing as a weapon to try and charm people out of their furs." Then I answered a call from a more cunning writer, who coyly said she had read somewhere that I'm gay.

"Do you plan to dance with men at the Opera Ball?" she inquired.

"I'll dance with anyone who asks," I replied honestly, "though I only know how to lead." I felt downright refined in my response, when in fact just a few weeks before I didn't even know men lead and women follow in a waltz.

"Really?!" she gasped, busily scribbling. "This would be the first time this happens in the history of the ball."

"Come on!" I laughed. "They do a dance called the 'Wiener Waltz'—I find it hard to believe I'll be the first gay guy to do it." I wasn't aware that the focal point of the ball is when 180 white-gloved Austrian debutantes are paired up with the country's most eligible, tuxedoed bachelors in a sort of graceful mating call set to Chopin.

The next day's headline: A NIGHTMARE AT THE OPERA: HE'LL SPRAY-PAINT THE LADIES & DANCE WITH THE MEN. Now the story had a life of its own, appearing in papers from San Francisco to Sydney. Television programs in Germany and England booked crews to cover what one article referred to as ANARCHY IN THE OPERA HOUSE. I sat dumbfounded at my desk and stared silently out the window across Norfolk's harbor in quiet southeastern Virginia, trying to grasp the impending, unintentional international incident.

. . .

It's a testament to Pamela's commitment that she didn't withdraw my invitation; on the contrary, she felt emboldened that we had somehow scored a two-for-one, having gained a platform to promote both animal issues and gay rights—or at least the rights of gay waltzers. Time after time, I've seen that what excites Pam most, aside from raunchy rock stars, is sparking debate about some of the serious issues that struggle for attention on today's mindless pop culture radar, such as domestic violence, AIDS, hepatitis, and especially animal rights. When PETA first heard from her, it wasn't through a publicist or a manager, but in a personal, handwritten note on lilac stationary. The return address, in neat cursive, listed the sender as "Mrs. Happy." Inside, it read:

Dear PETA,

I'm in a TV show called "Baywatch" and the press is obsessed with my personal life. I'd really like to divert some of the attention to things more important than my boobs or my boyfriends. Can we join forces? I've been an animal lover and a PETA member since I was a kid, sending in rolled up quarters, and I've always wanted to get more involved. Please use me.

Love,
Pamela Anderson

We soon asked her to appear on our first Times Square billboard, called "Give Fur the Cold Shoulder," for which she posed nude in a blizzard, her back to the camera but her head twisting around to give a smoldering leer. I walked into the sleek Century City studio as Pam was getting made up and was astounded by how the perfect natural contours of her face combine with the mesmerizing, unnatural contours of her chest to create a package that is utterly supernatural. Glancing farther south, I was surprised to see she was six months pregnant.

"Don't worry," she assured me with that famous smile. "Nowadays they can airbrush out a baby as easily as a birthmark." With that, she stole my heart.

Pamela told me that she was prompted to finally get in touch with us after an incident at a Texas car show for which she'd been hired to sign autographs. She'd heard some commotion across the hall and saw police run over to arrest someone shouting something about General Motors killing animals. She asked around and learned that a PETA protestor had handcuffed himself to a pricey GM prototype revolving on a pedestal and littered the crowd with leaflets exposing GM as the only automaker to still pummel animals in crash tests.

"I felt so frustrated, I wish I had known about the action so I could have helped somehow, even if just to bail the guy out of jail," she said. "I have experience in that."

After swallowing the lump in my throat, I cracked a grin.

"Oddly enough, that was me in Texas," I revealed. "We also took over GM's float in the Rose Parade, and they finally gave in, which was a big deal, as they'd killed twenty thousand animals while every other carmaker had moved on to crash test dummies."

"You're kidding me, that was you?!" she gasped. "Small world! But let's not miss each other next time."

By the time the faux snow was dusted onto her shoulders on the set, we discovered that we had a lot more in common than car shows and animal rights: we adore Elvira and Charo, we can actually duet songs from the rap duo Bytches with Problems, we've developed a similar open-minded outlook about relationships, and, most important, we're both extremely focused people who can't resist a good diversion. Often, you just feel like a colleague of those you work with, but once in a while the relationship transcends work, and you become best of friends. That's what happened with Pam, and we soon began synching our schedules to travel together, usually to promote PETA campaigns, and sometimes just for fun. We've traveled in cars that I've rented using coupons, stopping at Dunkin' Donuts for coffee, and in private planes she's finagled, stopping in Houston for the Super Bowl.

When Pamela was invited to emcee the World Music Awards in Monaco, she asked what local animal concerns she could address. I advised that if she met Prince Albert, she should encourage him to ban cruel exotic animal acts from the Monte Carlo Circus Festival, a PETA appeal that he had previously ignored. "*Meet* him?!" she replied. "He's my *host* for all three days—you should come along so we can pressure him at every meal!" Off to Monte Carlo I went. Over the years I've tagged along with Pam to Paris to show detached designers how two hundred chinchillas are electrocuted for one fur coat, to Milan to expose how conscious cows have their hooves and lips chopped off before being skinned alive for leather, to Florida to visit a refuge for terrorized chimps discarded by laboratories, and to Las Vegas to provide moral support when she unveiled her slot machine, begging her to declare, "I have the loosest slots in town." The *Times* of London did a magazine feature on our escapades. "Dan is my ethical adviser," she told the reporter, "which is as important as a hair and makeup person. Well, *almost*."

Pam traces her concern for animals to her childhood on rural Vancouver Island in Canada, where she often brought home stray dogs. One rainy afternoon when she was twelve, Pamela happened into the shed behind the house to find her father hacking the head off of a deer he had just shot. The deer was hanging upside down, blood spilling everywhere, and Pam screamed and cried so fiercely that her father vowed never to hunt again. Soon after, she stopped eating meat.

After high school, Pam moved to Vancouver, where she accompanied friends to a football game one day wearing a Labatt beer T-shirt. The game was televised, and a cameraman continually zoomed in on her. Whenever she appeared on the giant screen, the crowd went so wild that a honcho from Labatt found her in the stands and asked her to appear in their ads. More modeling gigs followed, including an offer from *Playboy* to come to Los Angeles to shoot their college issue; she made the cover. That prompted ABC to ask her to be the Tool Time Girl on *Home Improvement*, which led to an offer to star in a new syndicated series about lifeguards. Since she had moved near the beach, she took the part in *Baywatch*, having no idea it would become the most watched show on earth in the mid-1990s, and the first Western show ever to air in China. That led to other series and dozens more covers of *Playboy* and countless other magazines. Hugh Hefner refers to Pam as the most popular blonde on the planet, a sex goddess on par with Marilyn Monroe. Amazing, considering she never really auditioned for anything.

· · ·

"Mathews!" barked the brawny Austrian amid a group of watchful chauffeurs. I groggily walked through customs at Vienna International and wondered how the man recognized me without paint poured over my head. It was four days before the Opera Ball, and I had flown in three days ahead of Pam to try to change the public perception of us from nymphomaniac anarchists to lucid individuals promoting an important cause or two. I didn't think this would be such a challenge until I learned that Austrian movie theaters never showed *The Sound of Music*, even though it was filmed there, because people thought it was too kitsch and frivolous. If Julie Andrews was too campy for them, how must they feel about Pamela? I could only hope that times had changed.

"Give me your bag, and we must run!" As we sprinted to the car, he breathlessly explained that a pack of press awaited my arrival at a Moroccan restaurant owned by his boss, Mr. Lugner, who had promised a photo opportunity of me with him and his wife Mausi smoking the peace pipe, in this case a hookah, the North African opium apparatus. I could learn to like this Lugner. When we reached the parking lot's toll booth, there was nobody in it, so the frenzied driver leaped from the car and, looking like Hercules, lifted the guard rail so that we could speed out. All this excitement, and we hadn't even left the airport.

"Welcome in Vienna!" beamed Mausi, who was even prettier in person, with curly dark auburn hair and an outfit that looked just like the one Jackie Kennedy wore in Dallas, except yellow instead of pink. The restaurant, which had blue-tiled walls, was empty, except for my gracious hosts and a few reporters. This set the tone for the entire week; almost everyone I met, I met under the gaze of cameras, a jarring experience that made me appreciate my anonymity.

"Your flight was good, Mathews?" bellowed stout Mr. Lugner in his business suit with a warm, raspy voice. You can see some gruff tycoon in him, but you have to look hard, as on the surface he's very likable, with big friendly eyes and an easygoing temperament. He handed me a glass of red wine so the three of us could toast. And toast again. And again, until the paparazzi got their desired shots. All at once, we noticed that I was the only one who actually drank each time, and Mr. Lugner chuckled as he refilled my glass. We then sat around the giant Moroccan bong, and each took a hose; it wasn't lit, so we just pretended to inhale as the camera flashes went off. *Damn*—I've always wanted to try one of those things.

"*Wir können Deutsch sprechen,*" I offered. In addition to studying formal dance, I had polished up my meager German so that I would appear more cultured than I had been portrayed—and so that the Lugners, who I wasn't sure I could trust, wouldn't misrepresent me, Pam, or PETA in the flurry of media events that week. After a bit of banter, they seemed impressed, as well as put on guard; thankfully, one of the articles the next day was titled HIS DEUTSCH IS VERY GOOD.

"*Tanzen wir!*" squealed Mausi, giving me the signal to try my waltzing skills with her. We spun around a few times as Mr. Lugner hummed some symphony and played air conductor; it felt very Special Olympics but convinced television viewers that I was capable of dancing with a woman.

"It's a shame he's gay!" Mausi laughed to the journalists in her native tongue as I rolled my eyes.

"Mausi, I brought a little surprise for you from America,"

I teased. I just loved saying "Mausi." Over the next week, as a tension breaker, I would phone in the morning just to ask, "Is Mausi in the housey?" or in the evening to inquire whether "Mausi was feeling drowsy" and so forth. Anyway, I unzipped a garment bag and pulled out a full-length faux fur coat given to me by designer Marc Bouwer to present to her. The reporters seemed to like this setup even more than the bong pose, and the next morning most of the papers had photos of me helping Mausi, the Ivana Trump of Austria, who was known for her furs, into a designer fake. This impressed the animal groups, who were watching to see how I kept the issues in focus, as well as the ball-going socialites, who imagined me to be just brazenly antifashion (which I really am). Like an earnest Southerner, I aimed to please everyone; true Southerners know it's easier to get what you want that way.

The next morning I would need all the jetlagged charm I could muster, as I had a breakfast meeting with the grande dame of the Opera Ball, Elisabeth Gurtler, who also operates the historic Hotel Sacher. The Sacher, a Viennese landmark, has wood-paneled restaurants, rooms, and lounges, with walls covered in vivid fabric of different colors and designs, tulip-lamped chandeliers, grand paintings, and dramatic drapes everywhere you look. Some might consider the old hotel a bit overdone, as if furnished by Liberace himself, but I wouldn't change one sconce.

The history of the Sacher overlaps with that of the Opera Ball, which is held directly across the street at the Opera House. Both buildings were constructed in the 1870s, after

Vienna was well established as the music capital of Europe, home to Beethoven, Mozart, and other composers who popularized a magnificent new thing called a string section. The ball always happens the Thursday before Lent, when people in the Christian half of the world try to sober up so they can pretend to be more Christlike by the time Easter rolls around. In some places the daunting approach of Lent calls for a debauched blowout, such as Mardi Gras in New Orleans or Carnival in Brazil. Sophisticated Austrians, however, turned it into the year's most formal occasion, though it wasn't always as snooty as it is now. The waltz, originated by Johann Strauss, the world's first pop star, was the first dance in which couples actually touched and was considered outrageous when it debuted at an early Opera Ball.

Over the years, many less exclusive balls sprang up the same week at other venues—such as the Bon Bon Ball at the Konzerthaus—so that simpler folk also had a party to go to. But the Opera Ball is the sumptuous main event, and as such has been protested over the decades, even violently. During economic hard times, it has been targeted as an excessive waste of money, the epicenter of Europe's ongoing class wars. As the ball is presided over by Austria's president and other often extremely conservative politicians, demonstrators use the event to express outrage over wars, social programs, or other issues of the day. Police erect barricades to contain protesters a few blocks away, as they sometimes set bonfires and throw bottles.

What made our visit such a national obsession was that people thought that I might deviously bring the protest inside for the first time, with Pam's underhanded help—a radio host even suggested she might hide a can of spray paint in her cleavage. Each rebuttal I offered was dismissed with examples of other events I've disrupted. Although frustrating, it was strangely gratifying as an activist to be so notorious in a country where I didn't know a soul; sometimes it really pays to have a bad reputation. The experience gave me a real sense of career achievement and made me reflect on the global impact of PETA's audacious actions over the years and how we've become a true cultural force. Now the job was to turn the public's apprehension of PETA into appreciation for our concerns.

Mr. Lugner picked me up on his own to drive us to the Hotel Sacher, and I could sense his anxiety; the top morning paper carried an item that Madame Gurtler might ban him as well as me from the Opera Ball for turning it into such a travesty. For me, this created a terrific bond; we were no longer mogul and upstart, but a pair of subversives who had misbehaved and were being called before the principal, who might bar us from the dance. It gave me a warm and fuzzy feeling on this chilly winter day.

"Mathews, you must be more nice than ever when we meet Gurtler," he said, tapping his fingers nervously on the steering wheel.

"It'll be fine." I shrugged, gazing out the window at the spectacular palaces along Vienna's Ring Road. "If not, we'll have our own ball." He smirked and shook his head.

Just then, the news came on the radio, and Pamela's name was mentioned.

"Shhh!" he said, turning up the volume.

"Pamela Anderson discussed coming to the Opera Ball yesterday on the American talk show 'Tonight with Jay Leno,'" said the announcer. *"When he asked if she was planning to dance, she nodded and said she has been busily*

practicing the Vietnamese Waltz. Does she think she's going
to Vietnam, or Vienna?"

Lugner, stone-faced, took his eyes off the road and glow-
ered at me.

"She likes to joke!" I said. "That's why people love
her . . . at least partly." He whipped around a corner, stopped
in front of the Sacher, and handed his keys over to the valet.

Elisabeth Gurtler is every bit as exquisitely boned and
dignified as one might imagine the fifty-something woman
behind two of Vienna's most refined institutions, the Hotel
Sacher and the Opera Ball. Flanked by even more cameramen
than were at Lugner's restaurant the night before, she greeted
us at the entrance to her glorious hotel with a restrained smile
and a businesslike handshake. I kept hold of her hand, leaned
in, and kissed her cheek before we made our way through the
clicking cameras to a bright blue bar near the lobby.

"I know we have much to discuss," I whispered, "but I
can't forget to ask you where Beethoven is buried. My
mother, who is as deaf as he was, is his biggest admirer, and
she wouldn't forgive me if I didn't put flowers on his grave."

"I'd be happy to show you," Mrs. Gurtler politely whispered back, appearing slightly relieved. Reporters shouted
questions, which the talkative Mr. Lugner answered as
Madame Gurtler and I huddled to quietly converse. Elegant
servers brought carefully arranged fruit plates and tea.

"I'm very sorry for any worry we've caused you," I said,
looking her straight in the eye. "None of us, including Herr
Lugner, imagined all this would happen." She calmly listened, discreetly searching my face for traces of sincerity.

"Obviously, with the world watching, we have to make
points for our cause, but you have my word there will be no

disruptions at the Opera House." I stabbed at a few straw-
berries, wishing they had instead brought out the famous
chocolate Sacher torte, even though it can't be vegan.

"Thank you," she said, clasping my hand.

"So, *you* believe me, and the Lugners know, but how do
I convince the rest of the country?" I wondered aloud. "The
reporters just want a good show, but it would be wonderful
if they somehow addressed PETA's issues—and the ball, of
course—more seriously."

"I don't know if that's possible," she said. "But maybe
you could ask Alfons Haider."

"Who is he?"

"Alfons hosts the Opera Ball on the live national telecast—he is with the network." She sifted through a pile of
magazines on the table next to us and handed one to me.
"This is Alfons," she said, pointing to the debonair man on
the cover. "He was named the man Austrian mothers most
want their daughters to marry," she said. "But I think you
two might have something in common."

Our press breakfast soon concluded, and I told Lugner
that I would stay behind at the Sacher, as I had other business to tend to.

Vienna, straddling both Eastern and Western Europe, is
the city where Cold War spies converged to clandestinely
exchange information; the Sacher's garish café is exactly the
sort of place you would picture such a rendezvous, like
Zurich's Café Odeon during earlier wars. It has deep red
wallpaper and small tables, each adorned with a little coiled
steel stand that holds the menu and a newspaper. Although
tourists stop in, it is frequented mostly by affluent Austrians,
who subtly avert their eyes to scrutinize whoever is walking
in. Heads craned when Gurtler deposited me at a table near

the far corner. Before I had a chance to order anything, a waiter brought over a cup of flavorful Viennese coffee and—praise be!—a piece of Sacher torte. To be honest, it's a bit dry for my tastes, not nearly as tempting as a Krispy Kreme doughnut, but I ate half of it to be polite.

Twenty minutes later, the clatter of conversation throughout the busy dining room fell almost silent when Alfons Haider strode in, scanned the room, and sat himself down at my table.

"Well, you don't *look* like the devil," he said as we exchanged a firm handshake.

"Appearances can be deceiving." I smiled. Alfons is tan, trim, and smart, with the confident charm of a television host. We attempted to muffle our voices and restrain any flirting in order to have a semiprivate conversation.

"Madame Gurtler holds you in high regard," I said, "and judging from the stares throughout the café so does much of Vienna."

"They probably think we are having an affair." He laughed. "This week, they all know you as well as me. We only have one national television network in Austria, and we are quite easily scandalized."

"That's why I wanted to see you," I said. "I've tried to clarify things in countless interviews, but it seems the press wants people to think we're still planning some blitzkrieg attack, which we never planned in the first place."

"Yes, it has become a very exciting soap opera, it's irresistible, and reporters want people to stay tuned for the latest twist. Lugner is savvy enough to know that the more anticipation and sensation, the more attention he and his mall will get—but he isn't as concerned with promoting PETA or Pam so well."

"Right," I said with some exasperation. "I just wish we could use the opportunity to create a deeper appreciation for animal rights rather than just more outrage." The waiter brought more coffee. Alfons stirred in some sugar and gazed at the cup, in deep thought.

"There *is* one way you might win people over," he said pensively. "All of Austria watches one evening news telecast. If you appeared on that show as a live guest—alone, away from the shadow of the Lugners—you could make your points much better than in these edited segments, where you're at the mercy of the producers who show footage of all your crazy actions. Frankly, I didn't know you were so reasonable until I sat here with you. You should sit one-on-one with the country, through this show."

"That sounds like an amazing opportunity—but how can it be arranged?"

"The news anchor is my colleague," he said, wheels spinning. "I think I can help." Alfons pulled out his cell phone and called a bigwig at the network, alternately laughing and heatedly insisting that I wasn't merely conning him to get on the air and swing a dead rabbit, which was one of the latest peculiar rumors about what we might do at the opera. After making a few more calls, Alfons smiled broadly.

"Done!" he exclaimed. "A car will pick you up here at the Sacher at three o'clock to bring you to the ORF studio, which is in the hills outside the city. They'll have some questions first, but you're confirmed to be live on the national news this evening."

"Alfons, that's incredible!" I wanted to lunge across the table and give him a kiss, but this was Austria, not Italy. "How can I thank you?"

"You can thank me by meeting me tonight at eleven for

champagne," he said, scribbling down an address. "It's a beautiful bistro overlooking St. Stephen's Cathedral. But no dead rabbits, OK?"

En route to the station, I tried to focus on the points I needed to make, but instead found myself staring out the window, pondering how happenstance and the kindness of strangers can turn life into an exhilarating adventure.

The show went smoothly, no doubt due to Alfons's prep work; the anchor didn't fire off the usual accusatory questions but instead let me speak with few interruptions. I began with a friendly anecdote that Austrian concern for animals goes all the way back to the 1780s, when Josef II banned hunting in the royal gardens and opened the space up as the city's first big public park, the Prater (thank God for guidebooks). I beamed when I declared how thrilled Pamela and I were to embrace tradition by waltzing at the Opera Ball, yet also happy to call attention to some modern issues.

"Progress is the theme of this year's ball," I said, earnestly. "We hope that people will respect animals by not wearing fur and respect people by allowing them to waltz with whomever they choose, man or woman," I concluded. "And both Pamela and I are available, so don't be shy about asking for a dance."

It all came across in a friendly way, and by the time I got back to the hotel, several well-wishing faxes had arrived, many forwarded from the station. Among them, requests from a national gay group to attend their "Rosen Ball," from the candy makers to attend their Bon Bon Ball, from a millionaire with a sanctuary near Salzburg offering to send a car so I could meet him and his rescued pigs, goats, and horses, and a scrawled note from a militant local animal group asking me to help lead a protest outside of a Viennese fur boutique. Most interesting of all was a fax from an old hunting lodge near Czechoslovakia that had been turned into a vegetarian restaurant; the proprietors urged me to come sample their tofu wurstel, seitan schnitzel, and a veggie version of the traditional Austrian dish "deer ragout." Naturally, I accepted each and every invitation.

Overjoyed, I rushed into the crowded candlelit lounge overlooking the cathedral to meet Alfons; he too was jubilant about the show and led many toasts "to PETA and to progress." He introduced me to a diverse bunch, including an ever-smiling older gentlemen who ran a puppet museum, a tall, blond volleyball champ with his own sports show who invited me hiking in the forest, and yet more reporters. One asked if he and his crew could accompany me to dinner the next evening to film a segment on what a vegetarian eats in Austria; they kindly agreed to drive me almost two hours under a starry sky to the former hunting lodge, called Gasthaus Schilliger, near the Czech border, whose humble owners were delighted to have the exposure.

Incredibly, the tone of the national debate had finally evolved, and I was no longer talking about antics, but animals—and even veggie "deer ragout," a delicious dish that I never quite figured out.

About a thousand autograph seekers were expected to line up to meet Pamela on the main floor of the Lugner City shopping center on the day of the Opera Ball, but the clamor of the crowd suggested there were quite a few more. When Pam and I anxiously peeked out from behind the curtain, we saw people crammed elbow to elbow not only on the ground floor but on all three levels of the mall. The police estimated the crowd at five thousand, with thousands more trying to get in. An even more astonishing sight was Mausi walking out to greet the crowd and turning the event into an animal rights rally.

"Today is animal day at Lugner City!" she exclaimed over the microphone. "We have here Pamela Anderson to sign copies of her Go Veggie poster, with Mr. Dan Mathews of PETA!" A group of police officers led us out to a table set up on a stage. The crowd cheered and applauded enthusiastically, and those on the higher floors stomped, chanting "PA-ME-LA!" "PA-ME-LA!" For a moment I thought the upper decks might collapse onto us. Pam, wearing a tight low-cut black sweater, glanced up, waved, and smiled nervously as we sat down.

"Hi, so good to *meet* you," Pam graciously said to each awestruck fan, as the line of sweaty teens, giddy housewives, and cute toothless old men in overcoats began filing in across the stage for their six seconds with the world-renowned sex goddess. Many in the crowd carted nude photos from *Playboy* for her to sign, and a few even brought naked pictures of me at PETA protests for me to sign, which gave Pam a chuckle. All the while, Mausi kept the pep rally going by continually explaining what PETA was and why we're against fur.

"They even have a wonderful German-language website which you simply *must* visit!"

There was so much going on that we hardly noticed all the cameramen gathered at the base of the stage, until one of them let out an earsplitting whistle. Pam looked up, winked at him, then clasped my hand and thrust it aloft in a "victory" pose that appeared the next day in newspapers around the globe alongside a photo of the lettuce-bikini PETA poster and a story about our Austrian escapade. After half an hour it became clear that Pam would only be able to greet a fraction of her fans, and they grew audibly restless, so the police whisked us out a side door and into a big black SUV, where we caught our breath in bewildered silence.

With her straightened hair elegantly swept up into a chignon, and donning a vintage strapless velvet gown with long black satin gloves, Pamela indeed looked like Cinderella going to the ball. In my polyester tuxedo, rented from Casual Male on Military Highway in Norfolk, Virginia, I indeed looked like Potsie going to the prom. We sipped champagne and practiced waltzing one last time, around the hotel suite, to a Fleetwood Mac CD, as we didn't have any classical music with us. When the beat got too fast for the appropriate steps, we just laughed and spun around in a reckless embrace until we became dizzy and collapsed on the sofa.

" *'Tards!*" hollered the smiling longhaired man, looking dapper but out of place in his top hat and tails as he cracked open a Miller Genuine Draft. It was Kid Rock, Pam's then-fiancé. He doesn't really like Europe but changed his plans at the last minute in order to swing through Vienna to come to the ball—and to keep an eye on his lady.

"Everyone in Austria might know you're gay," Pam whispered with a grin as Stevie Nicks belted out "Gypsy" in the background, "but not in Michigan—Bobby isn't so sure." (Kid's real name is Bob Richie, and he's from Detroit.)

"It's just because I'm the first fag he's met who prefers rock to disco," I quietly explained.

Kid Rock is easygoing, and we share many low-class sensibilities, so I was very happy he came. He isn't much of an animal rights advocate, but he thought the PETA controversy added an exciting rock-and-roll element to the old-fashioned affair. We both felt odd wearing tuxedos, and we joked and cursed as we tried to adjust each other's ties. When a prim and proper security guard opened the double doors to politely hurry us along, Kid Rock was on his knees, fixing my suspenders.

"You just missed my giving him head!" he quipped.

As with Tommy Lee, I developed an easygoing rapport with Kid Rock via Pamela but we evolved as friends on our own, keeping in touch through wayward emails, the occasional concert, and a glass of Jim Beam when we find ourselves in the same city. We're all, in our own way, upbeat agitators, who express rage in our professional life but have a personal demeanor that's happy-go-lucky.

At last, Pamela, Kid Rock, and I made our way through the lobby of the Grand Hotel to join Richard and Mausi Lugner in a Rolls-Royce stretch limousine. Mr. Lugner told us it had been used by President Bush. The monster car crawled along the few blocks to the Opera House at the speed of a slug, as the roads were snarled by both ballgoers and demonstrators. The traffic made Mr. Lugner visibly edgy, which in turn made the rest of us a bit tense. In the distance, where the various protest groups were confined, a bottle rocket went off and made a shimmering arc low in the sky like Tinkerbell gliding down from the castle during the fireworks at Disneyland.

"There are my people," I said to nobody in particular. Nobody in particular replied.

Finally, we were close enough to the Opera House to see the gauntlet we had to walk; it wasn't just a red carpet, it was

a lengthy set of red-cloaked steps with hundreds of determined reporters swarming on each side and many hundreds
more spectators behind them. When the crowd saw our limo
approaching, the familiar chant began, with many of the formally attired press screaming like hormonal teens.

"PA-ME-LA!" "PA-ME-LA!"

"You guys, hold my hands and don't let go," Pam said
apprehensively to Bobby and me as we slowly rolled up to the
drop-off point.

"NO!" exclaimed Herr Lugner, holding up his shiny
white-tipped black cane. "We have agreed that Pamela enters
with me!"

"Never argue with a man with a cane," demurred Bobby.
"But we'll be right behind you."

When the limousine door opened, we stepped out one by
one into a bizarre abyss filled with glaring lights, screaming
voices, and the faces of anxious socialites who suddenly realized they were arriving alongside the belle and the beast of
the ball. And Bobby. It occurred to me that many people still
imagined we'd pull some stunt. My mind whirled with
images of all the things they expected us to do: strip, bran-
dish signs, toss dead animals, splash paint on someone. I
hated to let them down. Out of curiosity, I looked around as
we inched our way through the throngs and up the steps, and
happily, I couldn't find any fur-wearing targets (with the
exception of one cute old lady in a coat with a fox collar).

When we entered the fancy foyer, which was teeming
with swank society matrons and men wearing sashes, we
were amazed to be greeted with a smattering of applause.
Lining the jammed banister above was an eclectic mix of
approving faces, among them Madame Gurtler, Madeleine
Albright, and the chancellor. That's when I surmised that,

hopefully, our point had been well made. I started taking deep breaths, not to calm myself down but to fully appreciate the 45,000 yellow roses adorning the dazzling, buzzing theater. It was nearly impossible to decipher the questions being shouted as we shuffled along through the din, but I tried to appear dignified as I delivered a few statements. When everybody hollered at once, and it was pointless to try to reply, I just smiled, inhaled again deeply, and exclaimed, "It smells so *good* in here!"

Pamela simply looked around like an awestruck teenager as we were pushed along by the force of the crowd.

At last we reached our box, where we were greeted by a gaggle of aristocrats, socialites, and politicians—including some extremely conservative officials. Many of them gave me or Pam their cards, offering to help on pro-animal legislation. Once inside, with the polished wooden door bolted shut, we conducted our one proper sit-down interview of the evening— with Alfons Haider for the live telecast of the ball. He gave us yet another opportunity to discuss our issues with a few million people, and treated both Pamela and me as heroes; in fact, it was he, in some way, who secretly saved the day.

At ten o'clock, the elegant strains of Strauss started to echo down below. Pamela and I joined the Lugners and their extended family in a champagne toast, but Kid Rock stuck with his MGD. The lights dimmed, the fabled event began, and Pam and I became teary-eyed, especially at a beautiful number called the Tritsch-Tratsch Polka, which featured a chorus of children and a dance by Vienna state ballet students. Ironically, Pamela and I—the supposedly unrefined rabble-rousers—were the only ones in the box completely captivated by the actual show, as most everyone else was busy socializing.

Kid Rock, who spent much of the evening enchanting the youngest Lugners with a cappella versions of classic rock tunes just outside the box, popped back in at one point for another beer just as I was draining a bottle of bubbly. We laughed at our unlikely surroundings, and he asked at what point guests like us were expected to take to the dance floor.

"Not until midnight," I said, "just like *Rocky Horror*." Then I explained the gay scandal to him, saying that most people were probably praying that I was nowhere to be found when the waltzing began.

"Fuck that shit!" he shouted. "I'll dance with ya!"

On the day of the ball, the cover of the national newspaper *Kronen Zeitung* carried a headline about Bush and Saddam and a near-full-page color parody cartoon of Pamela, Lugner, and me arriving at the ball; I'm angrily swinging a dead rabbit, Pam is aloof and chomping on a carrot, and a stunned Lugner is desperately trying to block our entrance. On the day after the ball. the cover of the same paper featured an actual photograph of our arrival, each of us looking classier than we have ever looked before or may ever look again. "The gay paint thrower is actually a gentleman with outstanding manners," began the story.

Fortunately, a shrewd low-key Austrian businessman named Thomas Winger, who supports many of the country's humane organizations, took advantage of the official goodwill generated by the Opera Ball hullabaloo. He invited me to return to Vienna a few months after the ball to cohost a dinner in support of Austria's first federal animal protection bill, which had been proposed and defeated year after year. It aimed not only to upgrade and nationalize many feeble local cruelty codes but to outlaw the chaining of dogs outside with no shelter, to ban the use of wild animals in circuses, and eliminate the worst factory-farm cruelties, such as cramped battery cages for chickens, in which they can't even spread their wings, and tiny sow stalls used to immobilize pregnant pigs. I was asked to invite anybody influential I had encountered on my previous trip with Pamela. Alfons Haider instantly agreed to cohost the sold-out vegan dinner with me, and it received very positive coverage. Newspapers enthusiastically endorsed the bill, which finally won bipartisan support and became Austria's first animal protection law early the next year.

Lady Bunny.

CHAPTER 11

Ladies Who Lunch

"I want to meet her!"

"It's not really a *her*. It's more of an *it*."

"You mean he's had the surgery?"

"No, it has the plumbing of a man, and the voice of a woman, but the disposition of, well, I just refer to it as *it*, as in 'a class by itself.' "

Thus, I attempted to explain Lady Bunny to my mother.

We were in sunny Florida for Thanksgiving to escape the chill in Virginia, where Mom had recently moved to be nearer to me and the handful of others who indulge her at the PETA headquarters. Ma hadn't been in Miami since the 1950s and was curious to see how a rainbow had replaced the Star of David on local flags, so we booked rooms at the adorably dilapidated Dorchester for a low-key weekend reading by the pool or shuffling to the beach. The only real mission she had was to visit a salon for her annual yuletide nail treatment: pale red polish with snowflake appliqués stuck only upon the nails of her middle fingers. Invariably, some poor soul sees the sparkles, and to make small talk with an old lady, says, "Let me see your holiday nails!" to which Mom responds with a genteel, obliging double flip-off and a mocking "Merry Christmas!"

Our simple South Beach plans were to liven up, however.

Hobbling along Lincoln Avenue, Mom spotted a poster on a telephone pole for a party hosted by Lady Bunny, the razor-sharp queen of quips behind Greenwich Village's annual Wigstock drag festival. Bunny is also one of my dearest and queerest friends.

Delighted to hear that we were in town, Bunny had the party promoters send over VIP passes and a favor bag, which Mom and I poured out in a frenzy onto the faded floral bedspread. We ignored the lube and condoms, fought over the Stoli Orange mini, and exchanged an anxious glance after reading the event's flyer promoting some superstar DJ and a wall of bass-thumping speakers. Mom has to struggle to hear people with high-pitched voices, and Lady Bunny's is so high that Bun was actually employed by a phone sex line as a woman.

"This will not be a good hearing situation," Mom lamented. "Can't we have lunch with it instead?" I phoned Bunny back, and we made plans.

"I know from the stories that she changes her name more than the drags," Bun wheezed over the phone in a delicate Tennessee drawl, "so what does your mom call herself now?"

"She has been Perry Lawrence for the last few years," I replied, "but she also answers to Baby Jane and Mommie Dearest—if you holler loudly enough for her to hear you at all."

Most gays are highly selective about which of our ilk we'll expose our parents to, ever careful to showcase the most "regular" folks. Many homos would sooner reconsider pussy than set up lunch with their seventy-two-year-old white-haired mother and a gutter queen who still has a bruised nose from a rendezvous with a Gentleman Caller who refused to remove his belt buckle. But my mom likes people who treat every day as Halloween. She has been a drag enthusiast since *Some Like It Hot,* through *La Cage aux*

Folles, and right up to Pedro Almodóvar's latest. Growing up, my brothers and I were much more familiar with Divine and Tim Curry than whoever the current sports heroes were, and if there had been tranny trading cards, we'd have collected the whole set. My biggest concern in Miami wasn't that Bunny would be too much for Perry—or vice versa—but that they would both hold back out of awkward politeness and not be their true, sarcastic selves.

I first met Bunny in the late 1980s while barhopping in the East Village with Goldy Loxxx, during my years in his closet. Bunny, a go-go dancer at the Pyramid, lived in a rough walk-up, with skinheads in the apartment above who were antagonistic to gays, but for some reason liked their freakish downstairs neighbor. They were probably afraid of it. Bunny isn't your typical glossy female impersonator, but rather a scary clown drag, with multiple pairs of heavy black eyelashes and ridiculously huge blond wigs like an exaggerated Barbara Eden, a voice like a hungover Scarlett O'Hara, and the often-vulgar quick wit of Triumph the Insult Comic Dog. At Bunny's raunchy cabaret shows, a hand-scrawled sign reads MAKEUP BY SHERWIN WILLIAMS, CHOREOGRAPHY BY STEVIE WONDER, MUSIC BY MARLEE MATLIN. Bunny has an hourglass figure—though much of the sand is stuck up top. What you'll usually see is lots of shapely leg in opaque pantyhose topped by a large, distracting, garish blouse and flashy costume jewelry.

"Is there any topic off limits?" Bunny asked as we walked across the Dorchester's deco foyer to Mom's room, the clip-clopping sound of large Lucite heels echoing around the hotel lobby as if Mr. Ed were checking in. This question perplexed me, as Bunny had already prank-called her, pretending to be the Dade County VD Clinic, phoning to report that "over a dozen clients had listed me as a contact."

"He'd better come in quick for a test!" Bunny chortled before hanging up.

When we keyed ourselves into Mom's room Bunny screeched, "Hi-eee!" and hugged her, then stood back to give her outfit the once-over twice.

"Wow—where'd you get that dress?" asked Bunny.

"You like it? I got it at Lerner," Mom bragged.

"Hmmm—more like s*low* Lerner," Bunny quipped. Mom laughed out loud.

"Well, I love whatever it is you're wearing," Mom said, eyeing Bunny's green and red muumuu with a giant gold bow tied across the chest.

"I'm the Christmas present nobody wants to unwrap," Bunny replied in a fake sob.

"It really shows that you have a swimmer's build," Mom said. "Like Shelley Winters in *Poseidon Adventure*." The holiday weekend was off to a promising start. Perry was well prepared for Bunny, as I had been sharing stories ever since Bun and I fumbled into our peculiar working relationship years before.

One evening near Union Square, after Bunny and I were ejected by a movie usher because we couldn't control our laughter (the theater was showing a somber tear-jerker), we developed an idea about doing a PETA party at Love Machine called "Fur is a Drag." The event would feature a runway parody of a fur fashion show, with cross-dressing models wearing donated furs accessorized with leghold traps and paint. As the emcee, Bunny would ridicule each "model" on the catwalk with acidic, antifur color commentary. Many of the insults were self-directed: "This show has made me think about giving back my leather jacket—it looked better on the first cow."

We did the underground event on a Tuesday night, each of us snagging performers to participate, such as Lypsinka, Elvira, Deee-Lite, Hedda Lettuce, Mistress Formika, Mona Foot, Miss Guy, Julia Sweeney (aka "Pat") of *Saturday Night Live*, Flotilla de Barge the Empress of Large, and Miss Understood, who sang Gilda Radner's "Let's Talk Dirty to the Animals." Moby volunteered to DJ. The goal was to amuse ourselves as much as to make a point, but the response from the public and the press was so tremendous that clubs all over the United States and Europe wanted to have the "Fur is a Drag" show, offering to fly us in, put us up, and garner additional talent. At one of the events k.d. lang performed—for the first time all dressed up as a girl. She wore a flowing yellow chiffon gown, a tall brunette wig with curls, and lots of makeup, even false eyelashes; she was almost unrecognizable. The giveaway was her clunky pleather Doc Marten boots.

What I liked about this effort was that it boosted PETA as a good-time group, not dour and overearnest, as many causes are pegged. We worked it out so that Bunny organized the local drags, and I oversaw press and promotions. Soon, our little joke became a full-fledged campaign, covered by magazines as diverse as the *Advocate,* the *Face,* and *People,* and even by *CBS News.* In Paris the antifur soirée was held on the Champs-Elysées during Fashion Week and attracted trendy designers and stylists, and in London, the sold-out event was promoted by Boy George and featured the petrifying Australian performance artist Leigh Bowery.

It was a balmy late afternoon in Miami, and Mom and Bunny chatted as the three of us strolled down Collins Avenue to Gino's, a friendly Italian dive. I had stopped in earlier for coffee, and they couldn't change a twenty, so they gave it to me for free; since kindness should always be repaid, I insisted we give Gino some business.

"Is it safe to eat here?" asked Bunny, glancing around the sparsely populated dining room.

"Sure," I said, hesitantly. Because Mom and I are both vegans, I offered the dead fly on our white tablecloth to Bunny as an appetizer.

After ordering, we took in the beauty of our surroundings: Gino's is decorated with colorful plastic flowers intertwined with lots of twinkling white lights, draped around Roman arches and columns. The setting evoked a fond memory in Bunny.

"Does Perry know about our trip to Rome?" Bunny asked with a look that suggested both shame and glory.

"Oh . . . no," I said, pouring each of us some wine. "Tell it."

Bunny proceeded to explain how we were flown to my beloved Rome by the swank nightclub Gilda for a "Fur is a Drag" event. On the afternoon of the show, they had us host a surreal news conference, after which we went sightseeing. Bunny, in full Jayne Mansfield regalia, discovered that those ancient roads can be hell in heels.

"After we hit the Spanish steps, the Trevi Fountain, and the Pantheon, I was ready to change my name to Lady Bunion," it recounted as our food arrived. "But that didn't deter us from visiting the Vatican."

Thinking back on it, I'm amazed that the Vatican allowed us inside. Seeing gaudy Bunny hop into a nightclub is one thing, but watching it mince into bustling St. Peter's Basilica in broad daylight is quite another. Bunny, who was happy for the opportunity to give the hooves a rest, joined me in kneeling in a pew under the big dome in order to attempt a conversation with God. We're both dubious of the fantasy of Christianity, but wanted to remain open to a message from above, figuring that if we were ever to be reached, it would be right here, within spitting distance of the pope. To be clear, our question wasn't a strident "Why does your church persecute our kind?" or "Why would an Almighty allow such suffering in the world?' but rather a neighborly "Howdy—anyone home?"

We closed our eyes and concentrated, but nothing answered. With arms outstretched heavenward, Bunny assumed a pious pose, as if the glimmer of a gigantic plastic diamond ring might attract a response, even a bolt of lightning. Still nothing. We started snickering, and despite our best efforts, we were soon hunched over in the pew laughing uncontrollably. Because Bunny's cackle can shatter glass, even stained glass, the convulsing, bewigged jester soon seemed to draw more awestruck picture-taking Japanese tourists than the nearby Sistine Chapel. Just as in the movie theater, the authorities intervened, only this time it wasn't a minimum-wage usher in black polyester pants but the famous Swiss Guards, resplendent in their yellow-and-purple-striped outfits and over-the-top hats. They swooped in and escorted us not only out of the basilica but across the square and off Vatican City limits.

"Why is the pope the only man allowed to wear gowns in church?!" Bunny asked in a huff as the men brusquely hustled us out. This question met with a response as deafening as the simple query we had made of God. Fortunately, I was able to take lots of pictures, several of which appeared in *Genre* magazine under the headline LADY BUNNY'S PAPAL SMEAR. We were relieved not to be arrested and to make it back to Gilda in plenty of time for the PETA show.

By the time Bunny finished the story, Mom was in such hysterics that she had stopped even trying to finish her pasta marinara. Finally, she caught her breath and leered at me.

"Danny Lee!" Mom scolded. "How dare you visit the Vatican and not bring me a rosary!"

"Oh, shit," said Bunny. "Are you into all that?"

"Don't worry," Perry explained. "I was brought up in strict Catholic foster homes, but I always thought the Bible was just fables for people too simple to decide for themselves what's right and wrong. But I love the rosary beads! I have them in almost every color."

Bunny pretended to be relieved.

"Now in Norfolk I live in a HUD building surrounded by desperate Baptist widows," Mom continued, working up a rant. "Danny calls it 'God's waiting room.' Every Thursday night they have prayer meetings, and even with my deafness I can hear them down the hall, singing and making those asinine sheep sounds: *'We're poor little lambs who have lost our way, baa baa baa.'* And have you ever noticed how suggestive the lyrics are in gospel? Listening to my neighbors sing, it sounds like they all want to get laid by the Lord; they want Him *inside* them, He fills their *longing*. Since the church is against sex, maybe it's how they work out their frustration, but it's embarrassing."

"Ewww! . . ." Bunny laughed with a rare, shocked face.

To further prove her point, mom crooned an old hymn while batting her eyelashes and gyrating her septuagenarian frame in her creaky chair:

Have Thine own way Lord, have Thine own way
Thou art the potter, I am the clay

Mold me and make me, after Thy will
While I am waiting, yielded and still.

When you sing, you use a louder-than-normal voice. When you sing and you're almost deaf—and tone-deaf, in my mom's case—people can hear you clear across the state. As Gino's kitchen staff gathered in the corner to gawk at Mom sensually bellowing out gospel, each verse punctuated by Bunny's hyenalike snort, I figured it was time to walk up and pay the check. I wanted this heartwarming holiday scene, with family and friends bonding, to end on a high note. Plus, I was afraid that the waiter was about to come over and ask Mom about her Christmas nails.

Back outside on busy Collins Avenue, the sun was starting to set, and Miami was revving up for another chaotic Saturday night. As we arrived at the Dorchester, Bunny asked Perry if she'd had a nose job.

"No, but I'm flattered you asked," she said, taking Bunny's arm, not only out of affection, but for help in climbing the stairs.

"Wow!" Bunny marveled. "You must have been a real beauty—what happened?" Mom began giggling again and took forever to make it up the steps. For a minute, I thought I might have to stand at the top and wave a Zagnut bar to lure her to her room. Again.

The door was barely shut behind us when Bunny eagerly asked, "Do you think I made a good impression?" Mom asked the same question the next morning.

"You made a fine impression," I told each of them. "But I'll never again be seen with the two of you in public."

Show and tell at Harvard University.

CHAPTER 12

Bedlam

What to wear, what to wear?

It was the eve of my debut speaking engagement at Harvard University. I was at a Target in Boston with my assistant, Karla. We had been shopping for half an hour, and we hadn't even left the underwear department. She wondered aloud under the fluorescent lights if any previous speaker at the Ivy League institution had ever fretted so much about their underpants and decided probably not. I hadn't really thought about what I'd wear on the outside—certainly nothing too formal. In fact, I don't even know how to tie a tie. For this gig, all that really mattered were my drawers.

It hadn't started this way. At first, I merely received an email from a professor saying that some of his students had put me on their wish list of speakers for his philosophy class, "Personal Choice and Global Transformation." Simple enough. Then Karla read the attachments, which showed that the high-profile course, dubbed "Idealism 101" by the *New York Times*, was Harvard's second largest, with 587 students who met each week in an auditorium to hear civic-minded guests such as the Beastie Boys, the CEO of Tom's of Maine, former labor secretary Robert Reich, and linguist Noam Chomsky.

"I hope that the courage and exuberance of our speakers is contagious, and that we all may then be able to summon some of the same in ourselves," said the professor, Dr. Brian Palmer, in one of the many newspaper articles about the class, which was so popular that it swelled in size four times and had to move to increasingly larger halls. Professor Palmer was the university's soft-spoken lecturer on the modern West and head tutor on religion. "The emphasis at Harvard is too often on how to climb one's way to the top," he said. "I hope this course helps students think about to which purposes and organizations they lend their ability and, in some cases, their wealth. There are very few people who would say that what the world urgently needs is more investment bankers or corporate lawyers. More of us need to put aside selfish ambitions and deal with other, more urgent matters. Students tell me that this course, more than some others, helps them envision what they could become."

By now Ingrid had promoted me to vice president, though I'm not at all a "title" person. When asked what I do at PETA I usually just say I'm one of the hell-raisers. But seeing my name and title on this formal request from Harvard made me feel somewhat official. Plus, the email said that the students would get—as actual assigned reading—a few personal profile pieces, and some of the articles I had written. I instantly called my father, Ray, and stepmother, Joan, and they were overjoyed, which meant a lot to me. Although they have always been supportive of my work, I know it must have been a nice break for Dad to be able to tell his friends and my Jewish relatives that I was invited to speak at Harvard, rather than just hear from jovial cousin Jerry at Passover that he saw me on the news somewhere dressed as a carrot.

After I confirmed, Professor Palmer upped the ante. He

said that since class was at three, would I consider doing some sort of PETA action at noon so that the students could see firsthand how we operate? Action vs. words? Now *I* got excited. As it was still winter, I proposed that we set up a bed in Harvard Square and fill it with nearly naked people holding signs that read, FUR: OUT, LOVE: IN and handing out graphic leaflets. Passersby can't ignore nudity, especially when it's cold out. The students could observe how the flair you bring to a protest is as important as the issues themselves—if you want to reach beyond the small core of whoever might care about an issue and lure in the voyeuristic masses. Embracing this sad fact is what sets PETA apart from most other pressure groups.

The professor loved the idea. At the time, neither of us imagined this would mean that I, as well as Karla and several others—including one of Dr. Palmer's brightest students—would have a hard time making it to class that day because we'd end up in jail. Among the charges? *Indecent exposure.* In Massachusetts, such a conviction leaves you with the distinctive title of registered sex offender. Oy, my poor father.

Ironically, to avoid antagonizing the authorities, I had purposefully opted not to wear the blue Monopoly underwear I had found, which said "Go Directly To Jail" on the back.

"I vote for the SpongeBob SquarePants boxers," advised Karla in Target. They were bright yellow, covered with little Bobs, and best of all they were flannel, which would keep me warmer than the thin cotton Goofy shorts. Well, they'd keep parts of me warmer. Now we had to settle on Karla's intimates.

"I think my basic white bra will be fine," she said, rolling her blue eyes and resisting the trendy teen wear I was pulling from the racks and foisting upon her.

"Listen, you little bitch," I said in a mock hick voice, "you'll wear something girly and do as I tell you!" I only said this to see how nearby shoppers might react, but they didn't because Karla laughed before they could.

"Really," I continued in a more serious tone, "activists are often so dreary, and one of my lecture points is that 'cause people' should lighten up to make campaigns more entertaining, so we have to wear funny underwear." Although Karla and I have a professional relationship, it's often more like an irreverent friendship, which can make work seem like play. This is helpful when our work inadvertently leads to a misdemeanor. Or worse.

Karla's last name is Waples but we call her "Waffles." She comes from San Antonio, where she visited PETA.org to research a high school paper on animal rights one day after cheerleader practice. She soon became a vegetarian and upon graduating with an English degree from Southern Methodist University applied at our Virginia headquarters, where she was instantly hired. Karla is an organized, easygoing natural blonde who rarely wears makeup. But for the Harvard stunt, she did agree to wear the garish red-and-blue briefs I picked out. They had a cartoon monkey on them, dressed as Captain America, a look that perfectly complemented SpongeBob.

"I'm still worried about the permit," Karla said as we waited in line to pay. "Or lack thereof."

"We've done everything we can do," I said. "And the bottom line is, we'll be wearing more than some people wear at the beach."

A month before, as soon as we began planning our bare affair in Harvard Square, Karla called the permit office at the Cambridge Police Department and was told to fax a request, noting the exact time, location, and nature of our event. As we've put on similar events all over the world, we didn't envision any problems. But after sending in the request and calling the permit office every day for weeks without getting any response, we grew worried. Professor Palmer wasn't surprised; he told us that, unlike in the 1960s, when Harvard was a hotbed for demonstrations far more incendiary than our planned bed-in, the climate had changed, and provocative protests were not so readily accepted by the university.

Perhaps local officials were worried that Harvard Square would become a sea of naked Ivy Leaguers; news reports—first in the *Harvard Crimson* and then in the Boston and national media—speculated that in addition to me and my cohorts, many of the classes' hundreds of students might participate. Tina Fey even cracked a joke about it during Weekend Update on *Saturday Night Live*, which created a nice buzz around the country and terrific anticipation among Cambridge construction workers. The students were already learning that a little strategic exhibitionism can enable a small handful of activists with no budget to reach millions. But, of course, there might be some risks.

Karla refaxed the Cambridge police, stating that despite all the media reports, only five of us could fit in the bed, reiterating that we would set it up well out of the flow of both pedestrian and auto traffic, in a sprawling Harvard Square hangout called "the Pit." Again, we heard nothing. Finally, the day before our action, Karla received a call from an officer who told her that, after all, what we needed to apply for was a "public performance permit," and that it would take weeks to sort out.

"Sorry," he said curtly before hanging up.

In all our many, many similar experiences, we'd never

heard of such a thing. Local authorities are usually extremely helpful, even amused by PETA's antics, but it seemed that the powers that be in Cambridge simply didn't want us "hanging out."

"What are you going to do?" Professor Palmer asked me over the phone.

"Proceed as planned," I said, feeling a bit agitated by the situation. "We don't live in a police state, we have the right to get our message out, the girls are fearless, and I'll be wearing boxers, not ball-huggers, for Christ's sake."

"This is exactly the sort of determination I want the students to hear during the discussion in class," he enthused in his passionate, yet whisperlike voice. *Oh, yeah—class.* I had forgotten for a moment that the whole point of this was a sort of show-and-tell for college kids. Hundreds of them.

"I honestly don't expect any trouble from the law," I said, explaining the possible scenarios to him just as I had to my blasé bedmates. "But if so, protesting without a permit is a low-end misdemeanor, and we'll probably just get a 'cease and desist' or a citation on the spot—nothing that would jeopardize my being in the auditorium at three."

It must have looked like a slumber party breaking up when my comrades and I gathered that Monday morning in the small lobby of the Harvard Square Hotel wearing just our skivvies. It was a clear day, and not nearly as cold as it could have been. We came down a few minutes early in order to meet Kristin Waller, a sandy-haired, self-assured undergrad in Palmer's class who also wrote for a university magazine. She had decided that despite the permit quandary, the most interesting way to cover our bed-in was from a participant's point of view, by stripping and getting in bed with us, albeit with a pad and pen rather than a placard.

"That's the spirit!" I told her. "There's always room for one more."

A few businessmen dashing through the lobby froze in their pinstripe suits when they spotted Kristin and Karla wearing just panties, fiddling with each others' nipple pasties to make sure that no areola was showing; state law requires such to avoid nudity charges, and we almost always go by the book when going naked. Also meeting us in the lobby was Paul DeVido, a politically active friend from New York who had taken the train up to attend my afternoon speech and to drive the van full of streakers through the maze of one-way streets from the hotel to the Pit.

"All aboard!" Paul hollered with his head poked in the glass lobby door. "I've got the heat turned way up!" We trudged out slowly, making sure that we each had a sign and a pillow; props are crucial when you have no clothes.

Aside from Kristin and Karla, our bed was to boast fit PETA road warrior Brandi Valladolid, who has long, dark hair and a demure pout. When she appeared in a lettuce bikini on Howard Stern's show, he gawked and said that he wanted to marry her; she just looked at him nonplussed and continued her spiel about the "Lettuce Be Lean" vegetarian campaign that she was promoting to his millions of listeners and viewers. There were also two PETA volunteers with us: Aryenish Birdie, an unflappable college student who took the Greyhound bus across New England to join the romp, and Amy Thompson, a mischievous waitress from Lake Tahoe who was interning at our Virginia headquarters. When Paul stopped the van at a light, Amy seductively stared down a car full of guys in the next lane, and when she had their attention, she coyly slid away the heart-shaped pillow covering her chest and pressed her impressive boobs against the window. She widened her eyes and blew them a kiss when we drove off.

"How is it looking?" I anxiously asked into my cell phone in the front seat of the flesh-filled van, adjusting myself so that SpongeBob's "tongue" wasn't sticking out.

"As crazy as you could imagine," replied Michael McGraw, the modish young PETA director managing the chaos in Harvard Square. The Pit was crammed with several hundred spectators, among them Professor Palmer and his legion of students, Cambridge day laborers with disposable cameras, news crews from every Boston television station, and countless people who had stopped to see what all the fuss was about. Of course, what concerned Michael most was the swarm of police officers and the line of paddy wagons parked up Massachusetts Avenue, but we were determined to press on.

"Is it mattress time?" asked Michael.

"Yes, we're just around the corner."

"OK—it'll be set up in two minutes."

Because of our permit dilemma, we thought we'd be pushing our luck to erect an elegant four-poster king-size bed, as we had planned, because the police might surround it and block us from climbing between the sheets. At the last minute, Michael arranged to pay two guys from a moving company fifty bucks to wait up the street with a nasty, stained used mattress. When given the word, they would make their way through the crowd, plop the mattress onto the pavement, and cover it with sheets just as we burst out of the passing van and hauled our cookies through the throngs. Much of the bedlam in the square stemmed from the fact that nobody knew from which direction we would arrive.

"OK, gang—it's showtime," I announced as Paul inched the white van through bumper-to-bumper traffic and into Harvard Square. "Remember, this isn't an angry protest but an upbeat action, so no matter what happens, try to keep smiling. More people in TV land will 'connect' with us like that. And, of course, make sure your sign isn't upside down."

"Like Dan's often is!" yelped Karla. "He's all over the PETA training video in the 'What not to do' part!"

Spotting the van, Michael came up to greet us. He was surrounded by an army of camera-wielding journalists, but fortunately no handcuff-wielding cops. We pulled open the door and piled out, leaving the toasty van for the cool outdoors. People always think we must be freezing when we do these naked protests during the winter; in fact, your body manufactures so much adrenaline that you actually feel warm even in an ice storm (which luckily happened to me only once, in Amsterdam). As we hit the cold cement with our bare feet, we clutched our pillows and started the chant.

"Fur—out! Love—in! Fur—out! Love—in!"

We quickly made our way to the bed amid cheering students and reporters shouting questions.

"No questions till they're in bed!" Michael hollered back above the din.

Within seconds, the six of us were perched on the mattress, holding aloft our signs for all to see before we climbed under the hastily assembled sheets. It was elbow-to-tit, but I've never felt so relieved to get into bed. Because there was no box spring or frame to elevate us, it almost felt like we were on the ground, looking up to see only patches of blue sky through the flock of black humming and clicking cameras. Reporters had to kneel to talk to us about why we would "rather go naked than wear fur," and despite Kristin's intention to grill me on the mattress, she herself was busily fielding questions.

"I'm actually a student reporter," she told a writer from Reuters, the international news service. "I support the cause, of course, but I'm here to interview Dan before his speech in our class." Oh, God, I thought—class. I kept forgetting the purpose of my visit.

As I carried on with Reuters about my impending lecture, I strived to listen to the wonderful bunch around me, each of them making our case to the cluster of microphones in their faces. "We thought by showing some of our skin we might save some animals' skins," Brandi said to the anchor from NBC. "No, I don't wear leather shoes," Ayernish explained to the woman from the *Boston Globe.* "Are we cold? Come under the covers and find out," giggled Amy to a pack of breathless photographers.

After several minutes of unclothed cross-examination, the dutiful media circle around us widened, and we could finally see the mass of gawkers in every direction. Our original aim was to hand them antifur leaflets; we had volunteers throughout the crowd doing that, but I had hoped we could interact with them a bit ourselves. Instead, it was just us on a mattress on the ground in the Pit, with an empty moat of concrete around us lined by a circle of cameras waiting for something to happen, which was in turn surrounded by countless curious observers waiting for something to happen.

"I guess this is what it's like to be in a fishbowl," noted Brandi.

"I think we need to do something," said Karla.

"Pillow fight!" screamed Amy. The next thing I knew I was in the middle of a scene out of *Girls Gone Wild,* with pillows and pastie-covered breasts knocking all about. It was a memorable on-the-job experience, one that my heterosexual friends lament was wasted on me. Of course, it was this provocative image that made the rounds; *USA Today* trumpeted the story as a "Pillow Fight for Animal Rights."

As the busty battle subsided, a new circle of onlookers approached the bed. This bunch wore blue uniforms.

"All right—have you had your fun?" asked a dead-serious officer.

"Yes," I replied, catching my breath.

"You've got two options," he continued. "Stay here and get arrested, or leave immediately."

"Well, ladies," I said to my mattress-mates. "I think we've made our point; what say we split?"

"I think it's a good idea," said Brandi.

Michael instantly called Paul on his cell phone so that he could drive the van back around. But as we rose to leave, the press and the bystanders closed in, making it very difficult to move at all. We inched our way to the curb to wait for the van, but the crush of people was such that traffic started getting blocked. The police were not pleased.

"We really don't want to cause any trouble," I told the same ornery officer, who was trailing us with his squad. "Should we cross to the other side? It seems like there's a lot more room over there, and maybe people will know we're leaving." I had to shout to be heard.

"Yeah, go ahead—cross the street!" he snidely hollered back. With that, the goose-bumped womenfolk and I crawled our way through the slow-moving cars and crossed Massachusetts Avenue.

By the time we reached the other side, we were all in handcuffs, having been swooped down upon from behind by the police. The ladies looked like oblivious butterflies being captured by unruly kids. As most of the cops were dwarfed by my six-five frame, I looked like Gulliver being captured by the ambitious Lilliputians. Our treasured pillows plunged pathetically to the grimy street. The girls were not only cuffed but also covered up in ugly green hospital gowns that the officers had brought in bulk. This drew many loud boos from the crowd.

"Hey, what's going on?!" I asked in a bit of a panic. "What's our charge?"

"Jaywalking, for starters!" snarled the cranky captain.

At the station, waiting in line to get our mug shots, it looked like yearbook picture day at a nudist colony. The badge-wearing photographer and most everyone else working in the precinct seemed happy to have a break from fingerprinting and processing more hardened criminals—but not our arresting officer. One by one, as we were deposited back into the holding cell, we could see him in the office having a screaming match with the desk sergeant and others who questioned his grounds for arresting us.

"What are you gonna charge them with?!" a formidable policewoman shouted in her Boston accent. "Assault with a deadly pillow?!"

They couldn't get us on jaywalking because, as the uptight officer was reminded by a colleague, he had told us in front of several reporters that we could cross the street. They didn't try to charge us with protesting without a permit, as it would no doubt have been revealed that we had pursued the proper channels. In the end, two of the charges they opted for were fairly minor: disturbing the peace and loitering (on my form it was misspelled "Liotering," which for a moment I thought meant that I had unlawfully impersonated Ray Liotta). But these petty charges were just the appetizer. After some very heated bickering with someone over the phone, which we couldn't hear clearly because they slammed the office door shut, it was decided that we would also receive the more serious, though dubious, charge of indecent exposure. This meant that we would get sent through the system and formally booked before being released late that night— and that I'd be leaving hundreds of students in a lurch in the Science Center Lecture Hall.

"Well, this is one way to get out of class," I told Kristin, trying to make light of our situation. Getting a student arrested on such charges could lead to major problems, I suspected, depending on her sense of humor—and that of her parents.

"Honestly," I said. "I'm very sorry."

"Don't agonize over it," she mused, shrugging her sporty twenty-one-year-old shoulders under the untied hospital gown as a group of officers arrived in the holding pen to separate the ladies from the gentleman and whisk us all away. "I'm from Oklahoma, and I'm about the only one in my family who *hasn't* been arrested; this will give us something to bond over during summer break. Hopefully by then the 'registered sex offender' charge will be dropped!"

"There's no way that'll stick!" I yelled as I was led off to the men's wing, still wearing nothing but SpongeBob and handcuffs. Until now I hadn't really thought about the sensation my skimpy attire might cause in the men's ward. I hoped that I wouldn't be placed in a group cell. Once, after an arrest at a cattlemen's convention in Denver, my cow costume was confiscated, and I was deposited into a group cell of car thieves, 7-Eleven robbers, and drug fiends, wearing only what I had on underneath the cow outfit: sweaty jean cut-offs and a tight orange tank-top. To avoid being the bitch, I crawled under a cot and pretended to be asleep. Upon reaching the top of the stairs in Cambridge, I was relieved to see that I would be put in a solitary cell behind Plexiglas. The Latino in the cell next to mine kept bellowing questions about why I had no clothes, but I just ignored him and he eventually shut up.

For several hours I sat in silence and pondered my predicament. This is exactly what they mean for you to do in jail. The arrest itself didn't bother me so much, annoying as it was, but rather the fact that I was not making good on my commitment to appear in class. I may have an impulsive side, but reliability is everything to me; I never miss an appointment, a flight, or the opening weekend of a good horror movie. I hated the fact that the students had to endure all the assigned reading, only for the lecture to be derailed. Then I thought of the announcement they'd hear, that the speaker they had studied wouldn't be in class because he was arrested on indecency charges with one of their classmates—a girl, to boot. I laughed to myself in the cozy cell and soon decided that it was all rather glamorous.

Then I wondered what I'd tell my dad, who had been so proud of this impending Harvard gig. I thought back to when I was fourteen, when he had to get me out of jail after I stole Queen singles at Sears. I imagined that he'd just resign himself to the fact that things won't ever much change. I held out hope that he'd still be proud, in some way. Then I caught my reflection in the Plexiglas and realized that I was a thirty-nine-year-old man in solitary confinement wearing cartoon character underwear.

. . .

There were two banner headlines on the front page of the *Harvard Crimson* the next morning. At first glance, one might not know which of them related to the huge color cover photo of the vexed man being taken away by the police in his birthday suit: PETA PROTEST ENDS IN SIX ARRESTS or ESCORT SERVICE STARTS SLOWLY. In any case, the text was reassuring. Professor Palmer, when telling his class that I was still locked up, announced that he would invite me back to speak when I returned to Boston for my spring court date, and that because of the incredible national reaction to our little noontime slumber party, PETA would become a kind of case study for the semester.

It was the best jail hangover remedy ever.

Flipping through the *Crimson* in the shuttle van to the airport, another article caught my attention. It was an editorial lambasting me for "creating a three-ring circus for onlookers" while "failing to make a sophisticated point." It suggested that to turn people away from fur, we simply needed to share with them the facts about animal suffering, rather than make a public spectacle of ourselves. "PETA has repeatedly used shock tactics to further its cause," the column read. "It's saddening that Mathews will only present an extreme version of animal rights activism if Palmer makes good on his efforts to reschedule him. Mathews and his cohorts have done more to hurt the cause of animal rights than to advance it."

Rereading the column on my flight home from Boston to Norfolk, I became ecstatic about the amazing opportunity this critique presented. As soon as the plane landed, I phoned Professor Palmer.

"Brian, first off, thanks for defending me, and of course I'll be happy to speak when I come back for court. But I'd also like to organize another action before class."

"Well, it'll probably be warmer," he replied tentatively. "Maybe more people will go naked."

"No, I want to shift strategies. Did you see the editorial criticizing us for 'trivializing a serious issue'?"

"Yes, of course, but don't worry, I'm sure it's just someone well-meaning and idealistic."

"No, I love it—it's an open invitation for an Ivy League study of PETA's tactics. When I come back to class, it won't be to talk about what happened in jail, but what happens when we try to stage a serious demonstration. We'll gather in the Pit at the same time, with the same number of people, only this time we'll be fully clothed and carrying posters showing animals mangled in steel-jaw traps and being electrocuted on fur farms. I think it would be very interesting for the students to see the amount of public interest in a somber protest versus a silly one. Something tells me *Saturday Night Live* and CNN won't cover this one."

"This is perfect," Professor Palmer enthused.

The widely circulated news release about our more straight-forward demonstration met with a deafening chorus of snores from every media outlet except the *Harvard Crimson*. That paper pretty much just reported that few paid attention to the six of us holding up graphic PETA posters. When people looked at our signs, most quickly averted their gaze, strode faster, and refused to take a leaflet. It's not that they were unsympathetic, they just didn't want their hectic day darkened with grim reality. There were no bystanders with camera phones, no photographers from the Associated Press, and not even very many students. Whereas the absurd mattress melee was not just the talk of the town but caught the eye of literally millions of people across the country and around the world who saw it on the news, this respectable approach didn't even reach a few dozen individuals in person. It was the only time I was happy to have a flop; it set the perfect tone for my much-delayed appearance in class.

The crowded auditorium felt more *Oprah* than oratory; after Professor Palmer gave a comical overview, a teaching fellow hustled around the modern hall with a microphone like a talk show host so that students could ask the various devil's-advocate questions they had developed during their weeks of PETA studies. As usual with a formal lecture, I tried to remain oblivious to the lofty surroundings and to keep grounded so that I could speak honestly and plainly, as if I were chatting with friends at a party rather than rambling like a talking head on a Sunday-morning news show. The first question came from a group of feminists in the class, their spokesperson being a polite and plain nineteen-year-old from New York City.

"Why didn't you have more men in bed?" she asked, standing in the aisle several rows back. "Don't you think it was sexist to showcase so many nude women?"

"This is a common concern, and a good one," I replied. "First, as a fag, nobody wanted men in that bed more than me." This produced a healthy howl from almost the entire auditorium, which created an unintended air of disrespect for the student, so I carried on immediately rather than milk it.

"One problem is that it's difficult to recruit men for this sort of thing; women are often the only ones with the *cojones* to put themselves on the line for their beliefs. I've had this discussion with Gloria Steinem and she said that as long as we regularly include men in the campaign, she doesn't have a problem with it. The thing is, they never get nearly as much attention as the women do, probably because most of the news editors are men. But don't confuse *sexy* with *sexist*. I think that a lot of us North Americans can't shake our Puritanical roots and are embarrassed about sex and our bodies. I used to feel like this, though it may have been because I was fat before I became a vegetarian or because being gay causes all sorts of shame. It's actually quite liberating to protest naked, and most people tell us that they love seeing the natural human form used to promote a cause rather than a product."

She hesitantly thanked me and sat down, appearing only somewhat appeased. The microphone monitor dashed up the aisle to a young man toward the back.

"How and when did you start using these sensational tactics?" he asked.

"I've always thought that style should be as central to advocacy campaigns as it is to any slick consumer ad campaign. The whole naked thing took off when we learned about a huge fur fair being planned in Tokyo in 1992. The Japanese animal group wouldn't protest because they said that is considered rude there. Rather than let this massive convention go unchallenged, a daring friend of mine named Julia Sloan and I boarded a plane, desperate to figure out what the two of us could do on our own, with no budget, in one of the world's most expensive cities, to confront a multibillion-dollar industry. On a lark, we decided to announce that we were an American stripper couple who had traveled to Tokyo to do our act outside of the fur fair, with a banner that read WE'D RATHER GO NAKED THAN WEAR

FUR. PETA can't afford a costly foreign PR firm, so we went through the phone book and copied down the numbers of every media outlet and faxed over an advisory translated by some renegade kids from the Japanese group. The rag-tag bunch of us got off the subway hoping that even one local radio station might be there to allow us to speak up for the animals, but instead we found so many dozens of journalists that we thought the prime minister must be making a speech. They were all there just for Julia and me because we were going to strip. Julia's family didn't even know she had left the country. but they all saw her naked on *Headline News!* Amazingly, our little action became a top story all around the world, and soon other animal groups adopted the tactic in order to better put the issue on the map in their countries. Even the timid Japanese group stripped outside the following year's fur expo. What I love most about it is that it broadens our appeal to be seen as a fun group rather than just an angry one."

In the front row, a young man in a sweatshirt stood up.

"From what we read, you seem like a serious person— don't you worry that you won't be taken seriously when you protest naked or wearing a weird costume?"

"It is a worry, but I'd rather get across a light message than none at all. We're desperate to provoke public discussion, and sadly the media are more interested in sex and scandal than animal cruelty."

"But doesn't this dilute the message?"

"Yes, without a doubt, but most people don't want a message; they'd rather be entertained than educated, so we have to lure them in somehow. For example, how many of you came to the bed demo?"

Hundreds of hands sheepishly went up.

"And how many came out to today's more 'educational' action?"

Almost none.

"You see, there is so much competition for people's attention that you've got to be creative, especially if you are a charity with a limited ad budget. The reason PETA endures is because we remain painfully aware of what our simple society pays attention to. Sometimes that means we strip or wear dumb costumes or are confrontational. Other times we enlist celebrities, because a lot of people are more interested in a star's personal life than their own. I'm not saying I'm happy about this, but after our serious exposés are rejected by so many network news shows as 'too upsetting for viewers,' we have to do something to keep these issues on the public's radar."

It went on like this for an hour, and after class dozens of mostly sympathetic students hung out to ask yet more questions or just to chat. Among them were several girls who wanted to intern, a gracious Asian who insisted on calling me "Mr. Mathews," and a cool, scruffy anthropology major who gave me a thoughtful handwritten letter that said that no other speaker that year had sparked so much late-night discussion in the dormitories. He told me that although much of the scuttlebutt was about animal rights, the fact that I was so nonchalant about being gay helped open the minds of some of his homophobic friends and even prodded a few anxious undergrads to come out of the closet.

"Thanks," I said. "Always happy to help contribute to the delinquency of a minor." He laughed, and we moved on to discussing our favorite bands, like Flaming Lips, Grandaddy, and Goldfrapp.

When things finally started to break up, a group of theology majors invited me to dinner at one of Harvard's stately red-brick dining halls. I accepted, though I instantly started praying I wouldn't be asked to say grace. My prayers were answered; the only divine being I had to thank for my veggie dog was the nice black woman who put it on the tray. It was thrilling to see so many more meatless options than when I was in school. It was also oddly comforting to go back to a college cafeteria twenty years after I had graduated and still feel like the most immature person at the table.

An even bigger relief came the next morning in court, when distinguished Judge George Sprague appeared almost annoyed that our flimsy sex offender charges hadn't been dropped. He dropped them. Then, when the precocious district attorney made a big deal out of my similar misdemeanors in other states with the hope that I'd get a lengthy probation, the judge shook his head and refused; I just got slapped with a $300 fine. PETA isn't legally allowed to cover bail or fines, but I was able to pay by personal credit card. I also paid Kristin's fine and court costs because I figure inviting someone to jail is akin to asking them out to dinner.

The next morning, in a story amusingly titled "Legal Briefs," the *Boston Herald* wrote that "after much legal panty-twisting, a Cambridge District Court Judge ruled that protesting in your underwear may disturb the peace but it ain't indecent exposure." The *Boston Globe* ran two articles, and one of even them mentioned SpongeBob and reported that the ladies and I dined on vegan calzones after court.

This Notre-Dame gargoyle was about all I could see from my window in the psychiatric ward.

CHAPTER 13

Committed

Around 250 BC, a tribe of boat people called the Parisii settled on an island in the Seine in order to control river trade;
thus was born Paris. It was on this island—the Ile de la
Cité—that Jacques de Molay, the Grand Master of the
Knights Templar, was burned at the stake during the Inquisi-
tion in 1314, and where Marie Antoinette awaited beheading
during the French Revolution in 1793. On an unusually
muggy afternoon in April 2003, on the same historic patch of
earth, I found myself chained to a pole in the city's first public hospital and forced to prove my sanity. What's worse, I
had to do it in French, which, sadly, I speak with about as
much authority as the City of Light's most famous namesake,
Paris Hilton, speaks English.

Initially, when the young gendarme gawked at me in the
yellow-tiled cell, pointed to his head, and twirled the international symbol for "cuckoo," I thought he was being funny and
gave a nervous courtesy laugh. But an hour later, when several
armed cops burst in, lifted me from the blood-speckled bench,
cuffed my hands behind my sweat-drenched back, and hustled me from the precinct near place des Innocents to a hastily
arranged psychiatric test, I realized it was no joke.

The police van waiting outside blared its distinctive European siren amid locals and sightseers who had stopped on the cobblestone street to rubberneck the disgraced prisoner. They eyed me up and down, trying to find the gash responsible for the red splotches all over my white T-shirt and khaki pants and wondered among themselves whether I had murdered someone. I was shaking a bit, but I held my head high and tried to appear indifferent to the whirl of attention, like an awkward young model on a catwalk or a regal old collie crapping in a park.

Despite the siren, we weren't able to speed down boulevard de Sébastopol due to heavy traffic. I attempted small talk in English with my hosts but didn't get very far; two of them just chuckled, and the grimmer one simply said, in his native tongue, "We heard you speaking French so don't play dumb." The only comfort I found was from the robust black policewoman, and she offered only a kindhearted look, nothing verbal.

My chauffeur—isn't that what you call a uniformed driver?—pulled into the quaint courtyard of the hospital under the gaze of the brooding gargoyles perched high atop Notre-Dame, located almost next door. Our noisy arrival also attracted the stares of more puzzled passersby, among them a drunken bearded old man who looked as if he lived under Pont-Neuf. He watched sympathetically as I was pulled, still shackled, out of the van, and in a touching symbol of solidarity he clumsily punched the air.

"*Liberté!*" he bellowed with a scratchy voice, before the force of his own wobbly, flying fist caused him to lose balance and topple in a heap to the ground. Bless his heart; I wanted to buy him a drink.

The hospital is called Hôtel-Dieu, which means "hostel of god." It was built on the island in the year 660, and although it has been enhanced by many accomplished architects over the centuries, it still retains some grubby Gothic charm. As I was whisked through its stately doors under a bright blue sky, I reckoned that I couldn't be committed in a quainter place.

My wrists were fastened with steel rings and locked on to a small curved pole, which was in turn attached to a dark wooden bench in a busy holding area populated by all manner of marginal Parisians. Some had oozing wounds, and others were just wacky. To me, the nasal tones of the French language make it sound more eccentric than romantic, and listening to it spewed forth by those who were clinically crackers put me in a trance. I quickly snapped out of it when I considered that I was not here as a curious observer but as one of their peers. Though sobering, this wasn't a completely uncomfortable sensation.

First, when you are considered insane, you are no longer responsible for your actions. *What a relief.* Second, I've empathized with the deranged since I was a child, when my mom brought home poignant stories from her temp job at the Long Beach Neuropsychiatric Institute and took me to see *One Flew Over the Cuckoo's Nest.* I developed an even deeper sympathy in high school when I read a dictionary definition of *dementia*: "a mental condition in which one sees, hears, and speaks to individuals who aren't really there." This describes people in every kind of church I've ever visited, among them a few close friends. I learned patience early on for those who lose themselves in fantasy—and have even been known to appreciate an occasional hallucination myself.

Eventually, I relaxed my sore wrists and settled down. It would be a long wait to see the doctor who would determine whether I'd be spending the evening with old friends at a dinner near the Arc de Triomphe or with new acquaintances in a padded room. I took a deep breath and was at last able to reflect on the peculiar circumstances that had led me here.

Most Americans travel to Paris to marvel at the classic architecture around place de la Concorde or contemplate modern art at the Centre Pompidou. I went to incite a riot at Kentucky Fried Chicken. It was part of our ongoing effort to pressure fast-food chains to eliminate their most cruel animal-handling procedures. Only after aggressive campaigning did honchos from McDonald's, Burger King, and Wendy's agree to negotiate with PETA's mastermind on factory farming, Bruce Friedrich, and his colleagues, animal behavior expert Dr. Temple Grandin and professional mediator Steve Gross. McDonald's sweeping slaughterhouse reforms, which improved the lives of millions of animals, came about because we made good on a dare to distribute "Unhappy Meal" game boxes to kids in Ronald McDonald playlands. This popular item contained decapitated cow figurines and gruesome puzzles showing what happens to animals before they are turned into Big Macs and McNuggets. To save everybody the hassle of yet another campaign, we had tried talking to KFC before we printed even one placard, yet the company refused any meaningful dialogue, resulting in its own humane advisory panel resigning in protest.

We weren't insisting that they completely overhaul their business and use Colonel Sanders' secret recipe only on fried tofu, merely that they modernize archaic practices. As the powerful poultry trade was able to get birds excluded from the flimsy Humane Slaughter Act, turkeys and especially chickens are subjected to rituals sadistic enough to make the Marquis de Sade flinch. Without a law to cite, we couldn't appeal to the government, so our only recourse was to pressure the industry to act more responsibly, and KFC is the industry leader. Our demands were simple: kill the birds more efficiently so that they aren't scalded alive in defeathering tanks; adapt mechanical gathering methods so that the loutish workers one finds in putrid chicken sheds don't routinely snap birds' wings and legs like chopsticks; and stop pumping them so full of hazardous weight-gain drugs that their legs collapse under their own bulk. Hopefully one day everyone will have evolved enough to lose their taste for meat, but until then, the animals we chew up deserve at least some semblance of life as nature intended. Even chickens—who, animal behaviorists conclude, are smarter than dogs.

We launched our insurrection against the Colonel with a multifaceted blitz. PETA members across the country, including many brave souls in small towns, participated in "Why Did the Chicken Cross the Road?" protests. For this surefire attention-grabber, they staked out KFCs on busy boulevards dressed as chickens and crept into traffic in wheelchairs to give out leaflets. Comedian Andy Dick rolled one of these "crippled" chickens down the red carpet at the premiere party for his MTV series and explained to the media why he had a bone to pick with the greasy chain. Another MTV darling, Pink, posted the grisly details we documented in KFC's slaughterhouses on her popular website, along with a "Kick the Bucket" petition for her fans to circulate. The company wouldn't budge, but after Pink's appeal made the rounds, we heard from many thousands of youngsters who said that they would no longer eat any chicken at all.

As KFC markets heavily to the black community, we enlisted vegan hip-hop mogul Russell Simmons to back the boycott in full-page ads and drafted the Reverend Al Sharpton to host a graphic video exposé to be shown outside inner-city KFCs. In this video, which has turned away customers in droves, the ever-animated reverend concludes each upsetting segment with the quip, "KFC—that's foul!" Reverend Sharpton and Russell succeeded in bringing KFC to the bargaining table for the first time in two years, but the miserly company balked at making any significant changes, so it was back to the arsenal.

We next deployed PETA's weapon of mass distraction— Pamela Anderson. She wrote to the governor of Kentucky and asked him to remove the bust of Colonel Sanders from the state capitol on the grounds that it glorifies cruelty. The governor refused, of course, but nationwide news coverage of the "battle of the busts" drew several hundred thousand inquiring minds to PETA.org. To keep the pressure on locally, supporters in Louisville stood with Kentucky Fried Cruelty posters each Sunday outside the cushy fundamentalist church frequented by KFC's millionaire owner, Jonathan Blum, but the chicken tycoon just made like an ostrich and buried his head in the sand. The animals didn't have a prayer, so we had to intensify our efforts yet again.

When KFC opened in Paris, there was a predictable outcry over yet another American fast-food outlet invading France. This was an ideal sympathy to build upon, so we planned a major offensive. In order to make a splash that

would register all over the country, and perhaps internation-
ally, we decided to not just show a video and give out pam-
phlets, but to forcibly close the place down during a busy
lunch hour. A dramatic escalation like this might give the
cavalier chain food for thought. Because there is always more
interest in an action if a celebrity is involved, we studied the
local social calendar. As luck would have it, the Pretenders
were set to play a massive spring festival. The band's singer,
Chrissie Hynde, a PETA member since the 1980s, instantly
agreed to join the troops the day before her show.

Chrissie was born in the 1950s in Akron, Ohio, to very conservative parents. In the late 1960s, as an introspective teen,
she saw Russ Meyer's *Faster, Pussycat, Kill! Kill!* and soon
adapted the dark bangs, heavy mascara, and surly attitude of
the film's striking villain, a homicidal go-go dancer named
Varla. In the early '70s, Chrissie was enrolled at Kent State
University when the National Guard rifled down student protesters there, and shortly afterward, she fled Nixon's America
to England, where she supported herself as a writer. Chrissie
was among the first revelers in London's punk rock scene
and almost married Sid Vicious in order to stay in the country. Having taught herself to play guitar, she formed the Pretenders in 1979, and their first single, "Brass in Pocket,"
went to number one. After enduring the overdose deaths of
two bandmates and releasing several more hit albums,
Chrissie became a rough-edged cultural icon who was eventually inducted into the Rock & Roll Hall of Fame.

"I suppose this is an honor, but to me rock was always
more about being a loser than a winner," she said in the accept-

ance speech I helped her practice in her hotel room. But she abandoned it at the podium in favor of a blasé "Thanks."

My first "experience" with Chrissie was in 1980, when I played records one lunch hour in high school with my punk friend, Mary Fisher. Most kids in our sunny suburb preferred lighthearted artists such as the Captain & Tennille and Olivia Newton-John to upstart bands like Devo and the Plasmatics, and our guest DJ stint drew loud boos. Then we played the Pretenders' "Tattooed Love Boys," a sexy, jangly song Chrissie wrote about being gangbanged by some bikers she had antagonized in an elevator. After the lyric, "I shot my mouth off and you showed me what that hole is for," echoed around the cafeteria, students started throwing food at us. Our disgusted principal pulled the plug, and Mary and I had to be escorted out by security monitors amid flying burritos and milk cartons. I couldn't have imagined that when I grew up I'd be in an even more spectacular food fight involving Chrissie—in person—in Paris.

"We might have to go a bit over the edge to actually shut the place down," I told her in a softly lit wood-paneled café near her Montmartre apartment on the morning of our KFC action. "I don't expect this to be a totally peaceful protest."

"Fine by me," said Chrissie, a militant vegetarian since her teens. "My only worry is that I have to play guitar tomorrow, so I can't fuck up my wrist. If there's any hand-to-hand combat, I'll just climb on your shoulders again. Aren't you glad I'm not fat?"

Chrissie is the man we call when we need a street fighter. We've gotten into scuffles together in places as far-flung as Amsterdam, Cincinnati, Vancouver, and Washington, D.C. In New York, Chrissie led an occupation of the flagship store of the Gap, which had been buying cut-rate leather on the black market in India, where laws exist to protect cows as dogs are protected in the Western world. Ironically, Gap had offered Chrissie $100,000 to use one of her songs in its ubiquitous "Everybody in Leather" commercials. She wouldn't take their money, but she happily took over their window display and even pulled a switchblade on the mannequins to slice up their leather jackets. Chrissie, Ingrid Newkirk, my cohort Paul Haje, and the other raiders ended up in jail; the headline in *Time* read EVERYBODY IN HANDCUFFS. As I was on probation at the time, I was reduced to being spokesperson and bail daddy. Within days, Gap halted its Indian skin trade, prompting the governments in Madras and Mumbai to meet with PETA India and enforce their wonderful laws rather than allow corrupt local officials to take kickbacks from dollar-waving exporters. As a result, hundreds of thousands of worn-out cows were spared having chili peppers rubbed into their eyes and their tails broken just to get them on their feet to be smuggled across borders and turned into cheap clothing for American mall rats. All this, and Chrissie got out of jail in time for her sold-out concert at Roseland, where she dedicated one of her biggest hits, "Back on the Chain Gang," to her arresting officers.

I first met Chrissie face-to-face in the late 1980s, when I interviewed her for PETA's *Animal Times*. We began working on campaigns together, and I soon regarded her as a brusque older sister. I occasionally stay with Chrissie and her bright daughters when work takes me to London, and sometimes the two of us meet up on the road just for fun. In Boise on her birthday, we had a low-key "Strangers with Candy" marathon in a hotel room. Other times we're able to mix work and fun, such as in Brussels, where, after lobbying the European Union to ban cosmetics tests on animals, we had a wine-infused night of karaoke and ended up in some brawny Belgian's house halfway to Antwerp. He brazenly used the excuse of needing to moisturize his latest tattoo to take off his shirt.

As in New York, Ingrid was with us for the Parisian protest. She was being trailed by a crew from the BBC, which followed her to the Montmartre café so that they could be a fly on the wall at our preprotest powwow. Like me and Chrissie, Ingrid appreciates a funny, uncouth anecdote, especially in stressful moments, yet today we had to bite our tongues, as she'd had a small wireless microphone placed on her lapel for the day by the British field reporter. Those pesky hidden mics are easy to overlook; once or twice, as the three of us caught up over coffee, Chrissie and I began ribbing one another about some recent, unsavory personal exploit. Ingrid bulged her eyes and subtly pointed to her lapel to prevent us from blurting out anything off-color that might grab the attention of the eavesdropping producers and deflect from the purpose of the news feature.

"I can't wait to catch up over cocktails—*tonight*," Ingrid said with a forced smile.

We climbed into a taxi and drove fifteen minutes into central Paris, stepping out at place du Châtelet, a few short blocks from KFC, which was situated on a picturesque corner (it has since closed). Waiting for us at Châtelet was my friend Eric Ritter, a young, tan, suave, bespectacled French publicist I met at a party. Eric is always eager to take a break from organizing swank events for the Cannes Film Festival or Haute Couture Week in order to promote the latest provocative PETA street action.

"Hello, my friends!" Eric said in his charming accent, planting a kiss on each of our cheeks. "There are many journalists waiting for you," he continued, looking at all of us but really addressing Chrissie. "And there are some police, too," he said, focusing more on me.

We walked up the street and took stock of the crowd gathering for our noontime happening: a few dozen sign-wielding protesters (including someone in a chicken costume), a dozen or so reporters and camera crews, and at the outer edge, the usual bunch of dutiful cops there to keep an eye on things.

Like a soccer team skipping into play, we merged with the crowd and began the ceremony with the annoying chant "*Boycottez KFC.*" Cameras snapped Chrissie greeting passersby with our leaflets, and we all had microphones shoved in our faces. Whenever I do an action overseas, I learn a few key sentences in the local lingo, as those watching the news appreciate our message much more when they see that we took the time to learn their language. Sometimes, such as in Moscow, Hong Kong, Tokyo, and Rio, I've had to learn statements phonetically and find myself reciting them years later for no good reason. French is easier for me, as it's so similar to Italian, which I still retain from my years in Rome. I can actually do television debates in Italy, though in France I'm only able to express simple thoughts. Like, "*Le Louvre n'est pas mal, mais* j'adore *Euro Disney.*"

After the initial round of interviews, Ingrid, Chrissie, and I noisily pushed our way onto KFC's patio and barged into the crowded restaurant. We attempted to give leaflets to the startled customers waiting in line but were instantly pushed back outside the glass doors by a group of linebacker-like guards who had been rented for the day. *Quel bummer.* They took up position at the entrance to block us from trying again, while attempting to shoo in the trickle of patrons intent on getting their bucket of extra-crispy wings.

This was our cue to let out a Rebel Yell and try to scare all of the customers away. Ingrid reached into her loose pants pocket and pulled out a thin squeezable bottle of water-soluble red paint, which we glopped all over our palms. We applied it as generously as you would hand sanitizer after running your fingers through the hair of a homeless person. We then lunged for the entrance to smear paint all over the glass doors, chanting, "*Mangez les morts!*" The burly guards moved out of the way to avoid getting spattered, but after we clanged against the storefront, they quickly moved back into place. They grabbed us by our reddened wrists and repelled us back into the crowd. The police watched from afar.

"Dan, I can't have them twisting my wrists!" huffed Chrissie. "It's shoulder time."

With that, our KFC demonstration degenerated into an aggressive game of chicken. Chrissie leaped onto my back and shimmied onto my shoulders, and we charged back to the doors and the line of guards. At times like this, it's handy being six-five. We were blocked from getting through, but Chrissie was able to bang on the windows above our heads, smear more paint, and yell at those inside to get out. While the guards busied themselves with us, Ingrid snuck in around their legs, menacingly approached the counter with her "bloody" hands, and threw leaflets all around. The scene grew threatening enough to make most of the customers exit as quickly as their *petits pieds* could carry them. Now the police moved in closer, and a few officers bellowed at us to stop.

"Arrêtez! Arrêtez!" they shouted at those of us blocking the doors.

"C'est fermé!" was our response.

This became the new chant to advise the massive crowd gathering outside that the place was closed, and the protesters scattered up the block made sure that everyone knew why. Still, a few aloof individuals entered the large patio area ringing the KFC, and the guards squired them inside to place their order. I don't know who was more desperate, us or these coleslaw-obsessed Parisians. Eric, who was observing the scene from the sidelines near all the cameras, pensively approached me, much as a coach might huddle with a quarterback in the middle of an exciting game. That is, a quarterback with a shrieking tight end on his shoulders.

"Dan," he whispered intently, "I think that while their street sign and all of the tables and chairs out here are standing, it doesn't look so closed and some people will still go in."

"Excellent observation," I enthusiastically whispered back with a nod.

I backed up to a big green trash can and deposited Chrissie on top of it. One of the activists tossed her a megaphone and a French leaflet, which she read aloud to the hundred or so gawkers jamming the area. She looked like an animated statue of a war hero towering above the square on her platform. Now I was free to run amok and overturn all of the tables and chairs set up on KFC's patio so that any potential chicken nibblers would steer clear.

The clatter was deafening. As I saw on television later, I looked like a marauding maniac, like Godzilla stomping around Tokyo. Finally, among the debris, all that was left was KFC's tall, heavy red steel sidewalk sign, which I had to use the full force of my size-thirteen canvas clodhoppers to kick over. It smacked the cement with a thunderous gong—a gong that seemed to magically make cops materialize all around me.

A police captain, backed by several officers, got *tête-à-tête* with me and started hollering. But at the same time, a group of teens with book bags, who were riveted by Chrissie's spiel atop the trash can, pushed through and asked what was happening. I ignored the police and gave the students each a leaflet. Half-panting in pidgin French, I explained that because KFC refused to stop boiling birds alive, we came here to shut it down, and invited them to join us. They grimaced as they read the gruesome slaughterhouse descriptions and eyeballed the pictures.

"C'est fermé!" I started chanting again.

One of the kids, a girl of maybe fifteen with olive skin and dark curly hair, was particularly moved by what she read, and she quickly joined in the chant. Soon, her whole group was on the patio blocking the doors with us and daring anybody to enter. Watching their spontaneous resolve was among the most exhilarating moments in my career.

The crowd swelled so much that traffic on boulevard de Sébastopol crawled to a stop. This was the breaking point for the frustrated gendarmes. The police captain gave up trying to talk to me and instead turned away to bark orders at his squad.

The next thing I knew I was on the ground. Then, amid much hollering, I was hoisted aloft horizontally and spirited away from the scene by several officers. I've been swept off my feet by Frenchmen before, but never like this. There was a loud din of sirens and noisy chants and questions being shouted by reporters, but all I could really hear was the huff-ing and puffing of my handlers. They carted me off low to the ground, clutching my legs and shoulders and running down the street like they were competing in some odd contest at a state fair. I worried that my butt might scrape against the pavement, but they held me up with great skill. The invigorating sprint lasted three full blocks, all the way to the police precinct, where the raucous sounds of the street dissipated into sudden silence behind the metallic echo of a bolted cell door.

Other protesters, including Chrissie, Ingrid, and the person in the chicken suit, were given citations and released almost immediately. But the police captain was visibly upset with me. He told me that he had seen plenty of destructive behavior around Les Halles carried out by sloppy drunks before, but couldn't fathom why anybody in his right mind would wreak such havoc while totally sober, on behalf of chickens, no less. He said that he considered me a danger to the streets of Paris and refused to release me without a psychiatric evaluation. So, without divulging any details to Ingrid or Chrissie, whom I could hear making inquiries at the precinct's outer desk, he had me bundled up and escorted à la Hannibal Lecter to the Ile de la Cité.

In the harsh holding area at Hôtel-Dieu, a friendly nurse bid me *bonjour* and took my blood pressure. I exchanged glances with a few detainees across the hall, each of us speculating as to why the other might be here, but neither daring to say anything. As the hours trudged by, I pondered a dark thought: What if I failed the sanity test, whatever that was? What would happen next? Would I be restrained in a giant tub like

Neely O'Hara in *Valley of the Dolls*? Where would I be taken? Nobody knew where I was now, much less where I might end up.

I felt like the protagonist in a vintage Hitchcock movie: earnest American makes a misstep in a foreign land, and his life spirals out of control. I imagined that I was living most people's idea of a perfect nightmare—but the ever-curious tourist in me found the situation intriguing. It was certainly more interesting than spitting from the top of the Eiffel Tower. I might actually get tied into a straitjacket in a frightful French asylum—what day-tripper could ever claim that?

For some reason, things and places that disturb others often enthrall me. This includes clowns—the red hallway in my apartment is lined with thrift-shop paintings of them. I also find graveyards comforting. My ideal afternoon is strolling with friends around sprawling Arlington National Cemetery looking for plots bearing our names to photograph ourselves in front of. Once, I found a "Mathews" tombstone—with one *t* even—which I posed upon for black-and-white change-of-address postcards. Death in general has always fascinated more than frightened me, and I can't understand why people, especially those who anticipate a heavenly afterlife, don't want to be fully conscious to experience this ultimate adventure.

A second nurse arrived and spoke with my police escort. They unchained me and led me down a corridor to an empty examination room, where I was cuffed to a bed. This made me feel a wee bit more at home.

An open window offered a view of Notre-Dame. I stared at it out of boredom, and my mind wandered even further. I traced my path from troubled teen in the principal's office to middle-aged man in the loony bin, looking for some method to the madness. I reflected on the countless instances throughout my life in which people seriously thought that I was bonkers, mad, one sandwich shy of a picnic. I had to consider the uncomfortable question: Might I really be crazy, and it just took the French to prove it?

What would be my best defense with the doctor? Which explanation of animal rights would he find most lucid? The French can be esoteric, so I considered a peculiar sentiment once expressed by Mary Tyler Moore. "I don't want to be accused of being a lunatic," she said, "but I believe animals are the aliens that everyone expects to arrive in a flying saucer. We're all talking about what would happen if we met another creature who might have a different kind of intelligence, who might look very different, but who nonetheless does have a body structure and a spinal cord and who does feel things and can communicate with others of its own kind." Although I appreciate this notion, I imagine a converse concept. When I look at how sensibly the natural world has functioned over millions of years, and then think about how destructively humans have behaved over the past few millennia, it seems that we are the misfit species, insatiable aliens exhausting the planet of its resources and enslaving its inhabitants for profit and pleasure. On the rare occasion when I contemplate this aloud at a party, I find some people fascinated but get incredulous stares from most. Then I imagined how it would sound coming from somebody chained to a bed in a psychiatric ward.

Random events that I had previously considered innocent now came back to haunt me. I recalled the confused grimace of actor Henry Winkler, whom I once met at a cast party for a Broadway show. The famous black leather jacket

he wore as Fonzie on *Happy Days* was in the news for having been put on display at the Smithsonian Institution, a pop
culture accomplishment that many congratulated him on.
Then he was introduced to me. "I work for PETA," I excitedly explained. "We're always looking for ways to get people
to hang up their leather jackets for good—would you consider asking the Smithsonian to give us Fonzie's leather
jacket to use in our 'Cows Are Cool' protests?" His stunned
mug seemed to anticipate a punch line that never came. He
just looked at me like I was crazy.

I grew a bit forlorn on my little bed, surrounded by
police who seemed both baffled and bored at this point. Then
I recalled the most profound "loony" look I ever received. It
was a collective, jaws-agape gaze given to me by the somber
directors overseeing the Shroud of Turin, in the office of Italian archbishop Severino Poletto.

Let me first briefly set the scene. Jesus ran around with
the Essenes, a Jewish sect that shunned animal sacrifice and
meat-eating; thus, some biblical scholars contend that He
may well have been a vegetarian. So, PETA co-opted the
image of Jesus from the Shroud and turned it into an adver-
tisement with the headline, LEAVE A LASTING IMPRESSION—GO
VEGETARIAN. Rome's biggest paper, *La Republicca,* ran a very
fair full-page spread about our initiative, and I traveled to
Turin to launch the campaign outside the cathedral where the
shroud was on display.

Just as we started the unveiling in the scenic piazza, a
clutch of men in black approached. They were officials from
the archbishop's office, and they announced that we had no
proof that Jesus was a vegetarian, nor did we have the right
to use His image from the alleged burial cloth. The press

corps listened respectfully, mumbled among themselves, and then turned back to our poster-waving group for a response. As providence would have it, there was a tacky souvenir van a mere twenty feet away on the cobblestones, which boasted shroud coffee mugs, beach towels, mouse pads, and pens.

"Are you saying that they can use His image to make money, but we can't use it simply to promote compassion for God's creatures?" The reporters' heads swiveled back to the church officials, awaiting a clear response, but the clergy stuttered. Clearly not wishing to turn this into a theological pissing match, the officials invited me into the church for a private meeting. I left my Italian colleagues to finish up outside and eagerly went into the crowded cathedral, relieved that I had not sprung for a costly Shroud admission ticket the day before.

Once inside the grand Catholic enclave, we walked right past the actual Shroud, of which both the front and back are on display. I noted the splotches of blood where His hands and feet would have been. Then, to my amazement, I detected small skid marks where His rear would have been wrapped up. *Holy shit.* I was instantly thunderstruck. With an idea. The Ice Age man whose remains had recently been found in the Alps, was shown to have lived on a diet of only fruits and nuts, based on tests made of scrapings from his colon. The soiled shroud might well offer similar proof of its occupant's diet.

I could barely contain my zeal as I followed the anxious administrators up the dark stairs toward the inner sanctum. I struggled to put out of my mind any phrasing that might sound offensive, such as, "Here's how we can get to the bottom of this." Instead, as businesslike as possible, I pledged that PETA would spare no expense to fund an independent study of Christ's excrement, involving the world's most solid scatologists, to determine once and for all if He ate meat. Their faces contorted in ways that Henry Winkler's could only achieve after a decade in the Actor's Studio. The archbishop's henchmen refused the offer. I vowed to appeal to the pope, which I did in an absolutely sincere and scientific letter sent via Federal Express. Still no word back; I smell a cover-up.

Back in the Parisian institution, this stumble down memory lane prompted me to lighten up and laugh a bit. Then, hearing footsteps approaching the door, I quickly clammed up, realizing that laughing to oneself could be considered a sign of insanity. A fifty-something doctor, accompanied by a nurse, was ushered in. He was of North African descent, with deep brown skin, gleaming white teeth, and a thankfully easygoing temperament.

"So, what are we doing here?" he asked courteously in the language of his people's invaders. I calmly replied in broken French, explaining that I was an animal rights protester who had gotten out of control. I made the ever-important, can't-be-crazy eye contact. As I rambled, he nodded sympathetically and said that he admired Brigitte Bardot's animal activism.

"I think that you are not only sane," he proclaimed in front of the scribbling nurse and my police escort, "but that you are a good citizen." The evaluation lasted all of two minutes before he signed some form, shook my hand, and said, "You are free to go."

A few months later, safely back in the States, I received an exotic, official-looking letter from Paris. I tore it open to discover that it was a bill from the Hôtel-Dieu. For this once-in-a-lifetime detour through my mind, I was charged only €34.30, or about thirty bucks; here at home, this wouldn't even cover bus fare to Bellevue. That little slip of paper gives me much piece of mind, and I carry it wherever I go. Whenever anyone looks at me like I'm crazy, I proudly wave it and declare that I am certifiably sane. At least in France.

Perry during Bonnie.

Dismal Swamp Thing

"My Bonnie lies over the ocean, my Bonnie lies over the sea, my Bonnie lies over the ocean, oh bring back my Bonnie to me!"

My mother's wobbly monotone was strong enough to overtake the rumble of violent wind and sheets of rain hammering my silver Ford Festiva. Despite the risky conditions on this deluged highway, I was tempted to remove my hands from the steering wheel and cover my ears.

"Last night as I lay on my pillow, last night as I lay on my bed, last night as I lay on my pillow, I dreamt that my Bonnie was dead!"

"Please don't tell me you know every verse," I pleaded.

"Oh blow ye winds over the ocean, oh blow ye winds over the sea, oh blow ye winds over the ocean, and bring back my Bonnie to me!"

You never know which kinds of occasions will evolve into family tradition. Decades after my mom, while pregnant with me, snuck onto Newport Beach, hoping to behold a predicted tidal wave, we were rushing to Virginia Beach to welcome ashore another disaster: Hurricane Bonnie. Only now I was pushing forty, my mom was in her seventies, and the calamity was no mere threat. Speeding along on this dramatic August day, we knew that the eye of the storm was hours away, so there was still time to have some fun.

We arrived at the blustery beach in mid-afternoon, though it seemed like dusk due to the ominous clouds thickening above us. As Virginia Beach didn't expect a direct hit, many of the large modern hotels lining the artificially widened shoreline like ugly Lego creations remained open, though most were deserted. Parking was a cinch, unlike on most summer days, when tourists from both Virginias and both Carolinas pack this working-class resort. Battling soupy gusts peppered with sharp grains of whipped-up sand, we plodded headlong in our bare feet across the boardwalk and onto the beach.

As the outer bands of Bonnie began pounding their way ashore, we dipped our toes into the ocean's churning foam. That's all we really wanted to do. We kicked water at each other and raised our arms to see how long we could keep balance before grabbing hold of one another or toppling into the surf. After a few minutes of reveling in the angry Atlantic, we inched our way inland.

Mom, who resembled Medusa with her white hair blowing in all directions, stopped to write something in the sand with her toe. It was a name. At first I thought it said, "Bonnie." Then I heard her choke back a sob and saw that she was contributing a few teardrops to the torrential downpour. I reread the name she had scrawled: not "Bonnie," but "Donnie," her first love, in the 1940s, when she was fresh out of the orphanage and he was a young soldier. They nuzzled together at Washington's romantic wartime hot spots before he was shipped off to invade Nazi Germany, and they soon lost touch. Months later, as the Allies broke through Germany's western border, they found Donnie's body stuffed into a mail sack in a POW camp near Aachen.

By the time we were back on the boardwalk, marching arm in arm in order to withstand the forces of nature, Mom was all laughs again. Completely waterlogged, we latched on to a steel signpost to catch our breath. Looking up, we saw that it was one of the many anticursing advisories you see all over the conservative region. They have NO @&#$* printed on them in bold letters. Profanity in public is a Class 4 misdemeanor here, carrying a fine of up to $250, though many cases result in just a written warning, such as when a man told a cranky lady in a nursing home to kiss his ass. Reading the penalty on the shuddering sign above our soggy heads, Mom exclaimed, "Oh, shit!" before we scurried on to the car.

As a bicoastal connoisseur of natural disasters, I must say that living in Hurricane Alley is much more stimulating than living near a fault line. Earthquakes are all about the aftermath; there's no foreplay. With hurricanes, you get into it days in advance. You track the storm, tape your windows, gather up candles, and if it's less than a Category 3 and you don't have to evacuate, you stock up on bourbon and plan a party. Because hurricanes are given names, they take on an identity, and people spray-paint messages to them on their boarded-up homes and businesses, like "Bonnie be gone," "Ivan, we're thrivin'," and my favorite, from a construction site, "Wilma: Lay off our bed rock." This always reminds me of the playful pagans I studied in Rome who made similar appeals to their gods and goddesses of weather. The local news is fascinating when any kind of storm's a-brewin'. They show long lines of hefty shoppers stocking up on crates and crates of food and toilet paper, as if hunkering down for the seven hours it takes a storm to make its case this far north will cause them to work up an enormous appetite and speed their bowels into a frenzy.

Although Hurricane Bonnie first roared ashore well

south of us at Cape Fear, at just below Category 3 status, she surprised all of the forecasters by spinning around Nags Head and trundling full force into Virginia's Tidewater region. Maybe Bonnie saw Mom and me waving to her on Virginia Beach and, being a passionate southern storm, she wanted to give us a big wet kiss. Bonnie was an overnight guest who certainly left her mark. Giant oaks were uprooted as if they were weeds, roofs were torn off apartment buildings, boats were yanked from their moorings, $720 million in damages were racked up, 1.3 million people lost power, and I was finally able to finish a few hardbacks I had picked up in secondhand bookshops. One had a unique wind theme. Titled *Le Petomane*, it's about a celebrated Moulin Rouge showman in the early 1900s who donned a red cape and white gloves before bending over to perform songs such as "O Sole Mio" in farts. It's one of the few books I won't give away, sharing space in my case with autographed copies of *My Face for the World to See* by Liz Renay, *Vestal!* by Vestal Goodman, *Still Woman Enough* by Loretta Lynn, and *Wunnerful, Wunnerful* by Lawrence Welk. These treasured tomes are the only reason I got renter's insurance.

My favorite thing to do after a good storm is to go canoeing in the pristine Merchant's Millpond, at the southern tip of the Great Dismal Swamp, which straddles the Virginia/North Carolina border. Although hurricanes may be calamitous in the city, they are merely a forceful scouring in the swamp, where the sophisticated root systems that have developed over many thousands of years fare much better than the more recently erected structures in town. Paddling here on a calm blue morning, under a canopy of Spanish moss, among the lush cypress trees, with the only sounds coming from a red robin conversing with a green warbler or a turtle sloshing into his mirror reflection in the flat, dark water, it almost feels like the dawn of time. This paradise is also home to a variety of foxes, minks, and raccoons. When boorish fashion designers exclaim, "What would these animals do if we didn't breed them on fur farms?" I want to bring them here to see for themselves. More specifically, to drop them off on the fern-covered log where the patient six-foot alligator licks his chops.

I love it here so much that if I ever got a non-PETA email address, it would be DismalSwampThing. Although the imprint of civilization is hard to find in the swamp, it does have an exciting human history, mostly involving revolutionaries and alcoholics trying to evade the law. I'm inspired by both. Runaway slaves fled here before the Civil War, and moonshiners set up stills in the swamp during Prohibition. I retell their stories to any visitor I can lure into the canoe, including my awestruck niece, Paige, and my nephews, Mason and Grant. But the Great Dismal Swamp isn't only a refuge for outlaws; the place was named by George Washington, who tried to build inland canals here from Norfolk, which he thought would be the biggest port on the East Coast. Alas, the swamp proved too dismal to cut through, and the Erie Canal was completed first, making New York the major hub. Norfolk didn't really take off until the twentieth century, when it became home to the navy, Dollar Tree, Pat Robertson's Christian Broadcasting Network, and PETA. This makes for quite a diverse crowd at Happy Hour.

Why, you ask, would the nation's most unconventional pressure group relocate to a town so puritanical that the station airing *I Love Lucy* reruns refused to show the séance episode because it dealt with the occult? *Money, honey.* PETA's bright building on the Elizabeth River cost less to buy than our dumpy D.C.-area warehouse was to rent, and the cost of living is so low that even a nonprofit salary allows you to feel fairly middle-class among the gracious locals. I was able to find a large Gilded Age apartment with strikingly warped hardwood floors, floor-to-ceiling windows framed with a thick-grooved molding, and a wrought-iron balcony overlooking a quiet cobblestone street for $530 a month. Summer evenings on the balcony sparkle with fireflies and a symphony of crickets. During winter, there is just the hiss of the old radiator and a deep horn across the harbor signaling the end of the late shift in the Portsmouth shipyard. One winter, this horn also signaled the imminent arrival to my front door of an amorous, beer-loving dock worker in grubby overalls. In the Tidewater region, the pink triangle looks more like a blue collar.

"I read that Virginia receives four million tons of out-of-state trash each year," a friend told me at a dinner party in New York. "With you moving down, the tally will increase by two hundred pounds."

After residing in frantic world capitals surrounded by eager scenesters, I was very pleased to migrate south. Norfolk is so unpretentious that when an overflowing city dump was landscaped into a green hillside park, it was christened, simply, Mount Trashmore. This landmark, on which people push strollers and walk dogs, is occasionally closed by the health department when they detect noxious fumes seeping through its manicured surface, an unsettling reminder of the gunk collected below. But it almost always reopens in time for the festive fireworks display on the Fourth of July, where an old-timer once joked that a stray sparkler might just blow the whole place sky-high.

Ingrid did fret that we might lose some staff in the move, but all the principals came, including Marybeth Sweetland, the droll brain who oversees PETA's undercover investigations. She found a reasonable house practically in the shadow of Mount Trashmore. Thankfully, Jenny Woods, who works just a few desks away from me, also made the move. She found a modern apartment near the beach directly across from a bingo hall.

Jenny and I have been inseparable since 1988, when she was a young volunteer who tenderly claimed that she couldn't attend a circus protest one evening because she had to care for her sick grandmother. That night, I was amazed to find her swinging her mane of dark hair and dancing atop the seat directly in front of mine at a Mötley Crüe concert. Don't get me wrong; Jenny is dedicated. We've even been arrested together several times at demonstrations. On one occasion, when everybody was locked into a police van with their hands cuffed behind their backs, limber Jenny wriggled her shackled hands around her feet, pulled a box of American Spirits from someone's pocket, and placed a cigarette between the lips of each protester, including herself. The pretty prankster was in her seat with her hands back in place when the confounded sheriff swung open the door to unload the supposedly immobilized prisoners.

Jenny is one of the few people who will accompany me to Hooters. We don't go for the food—although I do love the fried pickles they occasionally have on special—but for the ambience. It's much like a drag bar, but with real girls. Once, a busty blond waitress sped around the busy dining area on a child's Big Wheel, slamming into people's chairs and throwing her head back in laughter before peddling on to ram another unsuspecting customer. They don't even make you pay a cover charge for this performance art. While it's not a gay establishment, I once received a memorable pickup line

at Hooters, whispered by a husky paramedic at the shel-
lacked bar: "You know mouth-to-mouth resuscitation? If not
I could show ya." During warm months, you can take a water
taxi from PETA's dock and get off across the harbor at Hooters Waterside. One year, the restaurant erected a billboard
geared toward enlisted men that featured a Hooters girl in a
belly-baring crop top and the slogan "Check Out Our Navel
Force." Alas, there were so many complaints that all the
Tidewater franchises had to agree to cover up their wait-
resses' midsections.

This leads us to the next local topic of interest: the military. Norfolk is home to the world's largest navy base, as well
as sizable army, air force, and marine installations. The
region has been a haven for recruits heading out to or back
from war since the sinking of the *Lusitania*. This means that
there is a proliferation of businesses where you can get an
arm tattooed, buy a prosthetic leg, or watch dancers shake
other appendages (a major thoroughfare here is actually
called Pleasurehouse Road).

One popular strip joint is JB's Gallery of Girls, where I
got to know a dancer named Allison. She has long tufts of
gently curled chestnut hair, the posture of an elegant horse,
and an Irish charm that captivates men young and old. I sit at
her little stage some Saturday nights and beg her to try new,
interpretive, and educational routines, such as one in which
she erotically checks her breasts for lumps. Despite my generous tips, she refuses. On her break, over cheap beers, Allison tells me funny backstage stories and makes me pretend
we're a couple if an especially pesky creep comes by. Most of
the patrons are harmless.

The only time I've ever been to a jail in Virginia was with
Allison—to bail her out. We had gone to see *The Bourne*

Supremacy one Friday night in Chesapeake, and as she squeezed into the aisle to make a popcorn run, she slipped on the greasy floor in her high heels and crashed down onto a steel seatback. She hobbled to the bathroom, dropped her drawers, and gasped at the swelling outline of what would soon be a bruise the size and color of an eggplant. Realizing that she wouldn't be able to dance for weeks, Allison fumed out to the lobby and drained her Irish temper all over the bewildered teenage theater manager, using a string of very naughty words. Unfortunately, a policewoman was there to observe poor Allison break that gosh-darned profanity law, and she was arrested. I sat in the theater for almost twenty minutes, wondering where she was. The dumbstruck theater manager was still quaking as he relayed the scene to me, and he shoved free movie passes into my hand as I dashed off to chase the siren.

Almost none of the many military guys in my circle of friends will go with me to JB's because they have no interest in spending their Saturday evenings gawking at women. Some frequent the handful of gay honky-tonks, while others, afraid of being found "out," attend small underground fetish parties. One such friend, who builds submarines, is heavy into leather. Although I find leather unethical, unattractive, and smelly, he and I enjoy each other's company. We even carpooled together to the annual Mid-Atlantic S&M Expo in our nation's capital; he went inside, wearing not much more than a leather harness, while I protested outside in the snow in rubber pants and synthetic cowboy boots, alongside a colleague in a cow costume.

Other gay servicemen frequent more conventional parties at houses or on boats. At one of these functions—on the vessel of a high-ranking officer—I had the good fortune of meeting the sardonic young John Machuzak. While some guys sought to ruggedly pose or preen, Johnny, with his hazel eyes darting all over the place in search of trouble, just provoked. When a flirty helicopter pilot approached him, little Johnny just tilted his head and said that he was too short for the airman. "I was born months too early," he deadpanned, his legs waggling from the Formica tabletop he was perched upon. "You see, I was a preemie—which explains why my skin has this bluish tinge."

Johnny and I quickly bonded, and within a few months he hung up his towel as a trainee with navy divers and became PETA's storm tracker. In this job, he monitors weather extremes all over the country and issues animal care advisories to the media. In winter, this means urging people to bring their dogs in from the icy cold, and in summer from the deadly heat. In autumn, he gets the message out to coastal dwellers to include their animals in hurricane evacuation plans. These radio and television bulletins helped prevent many animal deaths in the path of Hurricane Katrina, though we still dispatched rescue teams.

One of the dozens of dogs we brought back from New Orleans that was roaming the streets was a black teacup poodle, who, despite the hurricane and its aftermath, still sported perfectly polished pink nails. We named her "Fancy," and she became the overly cuddled mascot in our corner of the office. Fortunately, we were able to reunite the pooch with the lady who had fussed over her for years. The woman, who was stranded at a hospital with her amputee mother when the floodwaters rushed in, thought she had lost Fancy for good, but found her through a picture posted on the internet. She sobbed uncontrollably at their Texas reunion.

After more than a decade in the South, I happily consider

myself Southern. Because my mom grew up in Virginia, and because she gave me the middle name Lee after the Civil War general, I feel like I've got Dixie roots. Shortly after the move to Norfolk, I was amazed to read in an exhaustive biography that Robert E. Lee was an animal advocate. General Lee put fallen baby birds back into their nests during battle, severely disciplined soldiers who beat their horses, and had trouble eating rare meat because seeing the blood made him feel guilty. Of course, he's considered most noble for refusing to allow the conflict to degenerate into a reckless free-for-all guerrilla war, instead employing sharply focused strategic campaigns. I keep this in mind as I ponder how aggressively to fight my battles, having just returned from a blitz in some far-flung corner of the globe, sitting on my rustic balcony and glancing across the uneven cobblestone street to the white wooden mansion Lee visited after the war.

Then I consider the life and death of an even more inspiring Virginian: Nat Turner. With no army behind him and every force of society against him—as well as the subdued mind-set of most fellow slaves in 1831—he undertook the first major slave revolt. Nat and his handful of rebels wiped out dozens of slave owners before fleeing to the swampy backcountry to regroup. Sadly, they were captured, tortured, and executed. Nat was even skinned. Although the immediate impact was an even more miserable life for all slaves, his heroic effort sowed the seeds that led to John Brown's raids three decades later, which, of course, sparked the Civil War. Sometimes, when I consider the overwhelming odds that animals face, and the tyrants who exploit them, I feel like changing my middle name from Lee to Nat. I suppose I could settle for Natalee.

Acknowledgments

In addition to the many fine people fingered within these pages, I would like to thank Michael Selleck, Peter Borland, Nick Simonds, and Miranda Ottewell at Simon & Schuster/ Atria Books; Ira Silverberg, Carrie Howland, and Tom Eubanks at Donadio & Olson; Alecia Moore, Andy Tobias, Bob Sebree, Bruce Steele, Cassandra Peterson, James Brown, Jason Press, Jeannette Walls, Kate Pierson, Karen Porreca, Lee Knight, Jonathan Karp, and Todd Brown.

Special thanks to the Sterling Writers Room at the Portland Public Library in Oregon and to the glorious old Hotel Congress in Tucson, where much of this book was written.

About the Author

Dan Mathews worked as a dancing tree in the Disneyland Christmas parade and a burger flipper at McDonald's. He spent two years in Italy working as a model and actor before returning to the United States to earn a history degree from American University. Upon graduating, he took a job as receptionist at PETA and worked his way up for more than twenty years to become the group's vice president, charged with increasing awareness of animal rights through a variety of provocative campaigns. He lives in Portsmouth, Virginia.